SCREAMER to sweet dreamer

Lorraine Thomas

Hodder Arnold
A MEMBER OF THE HODDER HEADLINE GROUP

Cover © Photodisc/Getty Images
Imagetopshop/Alamy
Illustrations by Barking Dog Art

Orders: Please contact Bookpoint Ltd, 130 Milton Park, Abingdon, Oxon OX14 4SB. Telephone: (44) 01235 827720, Fax: (44) 01235 400454. Lines are open from 9.00 to 17.00, Monday to Saturday, with a 24-hour message answering service. You can also order through our website www.hoddereducation.com

British Library Cataloguing in Publication Data
A catalogue record for this title is available from the British Library.

ISBN-10 0 340 92820 4
ISBN-13 978 0 340 92820 2

First published 2006
Impression number 10 9 8 7 6 5 4 3 2 1
Year 2008 2007 2006

Typeset by Pantek Arts Ltd, Maidstone, Kent.
Printed in Great Britain for Hodder Arnold, a division of Hodder Headline, 338 Euston Road, London, NW1 3BH, by Bath Press, Bath.

Hodder Headline's policy is to use papers that are natural, renewable and recyclable products and made from wood grown in sustainable forests. The logging and manufacturing processes are expected to conform to the environmental regulations of the country of origin.

GET A LIFE!

SCREAMER to sweet dreamer

CONTENTS

DEDICATION

For Jerry, Ben, Josh and Holly, with all my love always.

FOREWORD

I have to confess I initially misconstrued the purpose of this book. Surely a book titled *Get a Life! Screamer to Sweet Dreamer* is about sleep techniques for babies and toddlers? How delightfully wrong I was.

This book is all about you. It's about me. And it's about any parent who wants to change their approach to the daily stresses and strains of family life in order to create a more harmonious home. The phrase 'Screamer to Sweet Dreamer' describes *our* transformation after following Lorraine Thomas's simple constructive advice for keeping our cool with our kids.

And, as many experienced parents will tell you, a cool parent is usually a greater role model than one who's all hot under the collar.

Being a positive role model for our kids is the underlying theory of Lorraine's work as a parent coach – a theory that makes perfect sense to me. If I yell at my kids, they yell back. If I'm stressed, they get stressed. If I'm not happy, they're not happy either.

Keep this book handy for those times – and they are inevitable – when family life hots up. It'll help you focus on the positive, turn down the heat, and enjoy being the cool, calm and happy parent you always wanted to be.

Now that's what I call a great role model.

Happy reading,
Mara Lee
Editor of *Practical Parenting* and mother of two

INTRODUCTION

Welcome to *Screamer to Sweet Dreamer.* Your adventure began when you became a mum or a dad. It's a life-changing experience that no-one can prepare you for. It's the most rewarding and challenging job you'll ever do in your life. It's definitely the most important.

As a mum or a dad, you hold your child's hand for a short time. You hold their hearts forever. It's a big – and exciting – responsibility. Every day brings new challenges for you to embrace, and opportunities for you to learn new things about you and your family. Our time with our children passes so quickly we want to treasure every minute.

Over the next 100 days, I'm going to take you on a fun journey that will give you lots of practical tools and techniques to help you deal with the challenges of family life. I'll also help you to become the parent that you want to be. There are lots of practical tips, too, from real mums and dads who want to share the secrets of their success.

I know you're committed to completing this journey with me because you're reading this book. That demonstrates the love you feel and your passion for being a great parent. This journey begins with you because you are your child's most powerful role model. Each step you take will help you to feel more in control of your family life. So let's do it!

I know you're a busy parent with a thousand things to do and no time to do them and that's why I'm making this adventure as easy as possible for you.

Our journey is broken down into 100 simple steps. Take a step at a time, a day at a time and by the end you will have reached your destination. Each day will help you get even more out of family life. It will help you to feel less frantic and to have more fun.

The journey will be enjoyable and inspirational. It will also be unpredictable. As a parent, you're skilled at embracing the unexpected – so enjoy the adventure!

CHAPTER 1

SCREAMER OR SWEET DREAMER?

DAY 1: INSIDE EVERY PARENT THERE'S A SCREAMER!

Inside every mum and dad there's a 'screamer' waiting to burst out. All parents know what that feels like. You're tired. You're stressed. You're at the end of your tether. And your child knows just what buttons to press to send you over the edge.

Being a parent is tough. There are times when you end up saying and doing things you wouldn't do if you were relaxed and calm. You're one of the army of parents feeling fraught and frantic.

We all know what it's like to have a child who screams. That high-pitched sound can cut right through us. But when it's us pumping up the volume, we feel even worse.

You may be an occasional 'screamer' or a frequent one. We've all been there, seen the DVD and have the T-shirt – although we never get the time to iron it!

TOP TIP

- Know that you're not alone. Most mums and dads struggle with the daily challenges of a demanding family life.

'Parenthood is part joy, part guerrilla warfare.'
Ed Asher, actor

Activity

Check your stress levels

Read the following statements and score one point for every 'yes' answer.

	Yes/No
• Do you feel stressed more often than you feel relaxed?	______
• Do you say 'no' more often than 'yes'?	______
• Do you have a 'to do' list that's never completed?	______
• Do you wish you had more time with your child?	______
• Do you feel tired more often than energised?	______
• Do you have problems sleeping?	______
• Do you shout more often than you'd like to?	______
• Do you say things you regret later?	______
• Do you feel guilty more often than you feel great?	______
• Do you wish family life was more fun and less frantic?	______
Total score	______

Your score

0–2: You're more 'sweet dreamer' than 'screamer'.
3–6: It's time to tackle important areas.
7–10: Life's too short to feel this stressed.

DAY 2: RECOGNISE THE SCREAMER IN YOU

The way you respond to your children will vary, depending on how tired or stressed you feel. Sometimes you feel you've cracked this parenting game. At others, you'll think family life is spinning out of control. There are certain times when parents say they're more likely to be screamers, including early morning, evening meals and bedtimes. Certain situations bring out the worst in parents, including shopping trips and car journeys.

As a parent, you're likely to be a mixture of 'screamer' and 'sweet dreamer'.

Screamer

- You're tense.
- You frown.
- You're enduring family life.
- You lose control.
- You're always too tired.
- You blame the children.

Sweet dreamer

- You're relaxed.
- You smile.
- You're enjoying family life.
- You're in control.
- You're energetic.
- You take responsibility.

You are your child's most powerful role model. So if you're more screamer than sweet dreamer, your son or daughter is likely to be too.

Activity

Sweet dreamer–screamer scale

Think about how you'd categorise yourself at the moment. Where would you put yourself on the sweet dreamer–screamer scale?

1–4: More sweet dreamer than screamer
5–6: Half and half
7–10: More screamer than sweet dreamer

1	2	3	4	5	6	7	8	9	10
Sweet dreamer									Screamer

TOP TIP

- Smile more often than you frown today. It's easy. You and your family will benefit as you focus on being more of a sweet dreamer than a screamer.

Real mum's advice

Listen to your child. I knew I had to do something when I found my three-year-old son cowering behind the sofa. 'I thought you were going to turn into a green, fire-breathing dragon,' he cried. It was a real eye-opener – and the moment I decided to take control.

DAY 3: CLOSE THE GAP

There's usually a gap between the kind of parent we are – and the one we want to be. That's normal. Most mums and dads would agree that they're happy in some areas but would like to make changes in others.

You can close the gap by answering these three key questions:

- Where am I now?
- Where do I want to be?
- What can *I do* to get there?

To close the gap between the parent you are now and the one you want to be, you must set targets. If you don't know what your target is – how on earth are you going to hit it? If you have a target, you can focus, prioritise and have fun hitting it.

TOP TIP

- Focus on one of your answers to today's activity. What can you do today to close the gap between where you are and where you want to be?

Real mum's advice

I was Basil Fawlty. I would get so worked up over little things and start ranting. I wanted to be Marge Simpson and have a laugh even when things weren't going to plan. Now, when I feel myself getting cross, I say to myself – 'Pull yourself together, Marge'.

Activity

Set targets

When it comes to setting targets as a parent, it can help to think a bit differently.

Focus on one word at a time and think about where you are now and where you want to be. Are you a cloud desperate to be a ray of sunshine? Or *War of the Worlds* wanting to be *The Incredibles*? Are you grey instead of vibrant red. Or is life so complicated that you're a chess game and you want to be a simple and fun game of 'Snap'?

	Where am I now?	Where do I want to be?
Weather		
TV character		
Film		
Colour		
Game		

Driver or passenger?

Are you a driver or passenger in family life? If you're a passenger, you're probably letting family life control you – and hoping for the best. Or are you in the driving seat, taking control and making things happen? Will you succeed in one of the most important journeys of your life – to become the parent you want to be?

I know that you will succeed if you want to. You've told me a lot about yourself, just by wanting to read this book. You know that being a mum or dad is rewarding. You also know just how challenging it can be. You know that you hold your child's hand for a short while but their heart forever. You want to make the most of your time with them and be the best parent you can be. You're a 'can do' parent rather than a 'can't do' parent. You find reasons to succeed, rather than excuses not to.

TOP TIP

- Read the success list from today's activity out loud to yourself every night. Believe in yourself. Go to sleep knowing that you're going to reach your destination.

Activity

Rate your successes

Read the following statements and score one point for every 'yes'.

	Yes/No
• I'm passionate about being a parent.	________
• I'm doing the most important job I'll do in my life.	________
• I want to invest time.	________
• I want to invest energy.	________
• I'm committed to success.	________
• I'm determined to achieve my goal.	________
• I want to make my development as a parent my priority.	________
• I want to be the best parent I can be.	________
• I'm going to enjoy this adventure.	________
• I'm going to succeed.	________
Total score	________

Your success rating

0–3: You lack the commitment to succeed.

4–6: You can do this but only if you really want to.

7+: You'll definitely succeed.

Get a life… not a lunch-box

It's easy to fall into the trap of taking your relationship with your child for granted. There are always so many other things that need your attention – right now! You can be far too busy changing nappies, hunting for a pair of matching socks or desperately trying to find something healthy to put in their nursery lunch-box to be thinking about life.

But you're different. You want to think about life instead of that lunch-box and you're determined to. Today is a defining moment in your life as a parent. You're on an exciting adventure to become the mum or dad you want to be. You know what you want and you're committed to making it happen.

Every day will take you one step closer to reaching your destination. You're motivated. You're looking forward. You know where you want to go. All great relationships need working at. They don't just happen. That's particularly true of your relationship with your child. As you invest your love and time and energy, your relationship will grow stronger.

TOP TIP

- Celebrate every day as a *new* and *exciting* opportunity to make a positive difference to your child's life.

Real mum's advice

It was my daughter's first day at school. There were tears – mine. I couldn't believe that she was nearly five. Where had the years gone? It made me determined to treasure every day I had with her from now on.

Activity

Commit to your contract

Read and sign the following contract.

Screamer to Sweet Dreamer Contract

1. I'm passionate about being a parent.
2. I'm ready to take control.
3. I want to invest time and energy.
4. I'm committed to success.
5. I'm motivated to achieve my goal.
6. I want to develop as a parent.
7. I want to be the best parent I can be.
8. I'm going to enjoy this adventure.
9. I will close the gap between the parent I am now and the one I want to be.
10. I'm going to succeed.

Date: ______________

Your signature: __________________________

Your notes

CHAPTER 2

BE THE PARENT YOU WANT TO BE

You are your child's most powerful role model and with that power comes great responsibility. Enjoy that responsibility. At times it may seem overwhelming, but it means you can have an amazing impact on your child.

Everything you do or say:

- affects the way they behave
- affects their relationships
- influences their development
- affects the person they grow up to be
- colours their view of the world.

Activity

Mantra time

Say aloud to yourself, 'I'm my child's most powerful role model'. Spend time today focusing on yourself as a role model. Be aware of how you behave and what you do and say.

Give yourself a role model MOT. Here are three specific areas for you to focus on. What kind of a role model do you provide for your child?

- **Mealtimes** You want your child to eat a healthy, balanced diet. But are you?
- **Television** You don't want your child to watch too much TV. But are you?
- **Challenges** You want your child to deal calmly and positively with challenges. But are you?

TOP TIP

- See what you do through your child's eyes. This is the best way to understand what powerful messages you are sending them.

'What a child doesn't receive he can seldom later give.'
P.D. James, author

Real dad's advice

I'm a big sports fan, but when I saw a picture that my three-year-old had drawn at nursery, it was a real shock and made me take a long hard look at my habits. The picture showed me in front of the TV, mum in the kitchen and our daughter playing on her own.

DAY 7: RATE YOURSELF AS A ROLE MODEL

You are your child's most powerful role model. You will affect the way your child develops. You can be a positive role model or a negative one.

Positive role model

If you're a positive 'can do' parent who embraces challenges and enjoys family life, your child is likely to as well.

Negative role model

If you're a negative 'can't do' parent who is always finding problems, your child is likely to too.

Three great reasons to be a positive role model

1 You'll be happy and motivated.
2 Your child will grow up excited about the adventure of life.
3 Your child is much more likely to stay out of trouble as a teenager.

TOP TIP

- No matter how challenging it might be – always act your age not theirs! Don't take your lead from them. You're the adult. Let them learn from you.

Activity

How do you rate yourself as a role model?

In each line of the table, write down something that you do well. Each positive skill or quality scores you a mark out of ten. You may not be used to focusing on your good bits – so break the habit of a lifetime and score as many points as you can.

	I'm a good role model for my child because	Score
1.		
2.		
3.		
4.		
5.		
6.		
7.		
8.		
9.		
10.		
	Total score	

Your score

0–4: A low score but don't worry. It's important to be honest. There's lots of room for improvement – and you've taken the first step by recognising this.

5–7: Good for you. You're doing well in the role model department.

8–10: Excellent. Enjoy improving on perfection!

Being the parent you want to be means exactly that. It means being the parent *you* want to be – not the parent *other people* want you to be. You're the expert in your own situation so go with your gut instinct.

Tune into your child

Parents have a great gut instinct. Imagine your child is screaming, for example. If you 'tune' into them – you'll nearly always know what they're trying to tell you. It may be your baby crying, your toddler throwing a tantrum or your teenager having a turn. They're sending you a powerful message. Don't take it personally. It's not about you. It's about them.

The same is true about you. Remember that when you're raising your voice with your child or saying things you wouldn't do when you are calm – you're sending them a powerful message about you. It's not about them.

TOP TIP

If your gut instinct is to deal with the challenge yourself, do it today. If your gut instinct is to get support and advice, get it today.

- Speak to your health visitor, GP or call the NHS Helpline.
- Find out about local support groups in your area.
- Contact a charity like Parentalk (www.parentalk.co.uk).
- Surf the web to get more information and contacts.
- Buy a great magazine on parenting like *Practical Parenting*.
- Read a good book on the subject.

'The most important thing I've learned over the years is that there is no way to be a perfect mother and a million ways to be a good one.'
Jill Churchill, writer

Activity

Work out the reasons for screaming

Your child will scream for a reason. Below are some of the most common ones. Circle 'Yes' or 'No' to indicate that you can recognise these in your own child. Score one point for each 'Yes'.

- They're bored. Yes/No
- They're hungry. Yes/No
- They're tired. Yes/No
- They want their own way. Yes/No
- They want your attention. Yes/No
- They're in pain. Yes/No
- They're frustrated. Yes/No
- They're anxious. Yes/No

What's your 'gut instinct' rating out of 8?

The title of this chapter is 'be the parent you want to be'. That means having the confidence to be the parent *you want* to be – not the parent that other people want you to be.

If you think you can, you will. If you think you can't, you'll be absolutely right. So decide today to be the parent *you want* to be – and you will.

Different types of confidence

There are two different types of confidence.

Weak outer confidence

- Dependent on what other people say about you
- Affected by what you think other people think about you
- Dependent on other people, e.g. family, friends, teachers, etc.
- Outside your control = weak confidence

Strong inner confidence

- Dependent on what you say about you
- Not affected by what you think other people think about you
- Dependent on you, not other people
- Inside your control = strong confidence

Create a 'can do' child

You can't always be with your child, but you can help them develop the inner confidence to say 'no' when they want to. Your child may be tiny now, but boosting that inner confidence will give them the courage to say 'no' to drink, drugs and getting into trouble when they're teenagers. Start today and you can give them the confidence to be the person they want to be – not the person others want them to be.

Activity

Find confidence-boosting activities

Choose one of today's top tips and use it to boost your child's inner confidence today.

TOP TIP

- Go on a 'feeling–finding' mission and encourage your child to talk about what they do well and how it feels.
- Smile more often than you frown – your child will feel valued and secure.
- Challenge them when they say 'I can't' or 'I'm no good at that'. Help them to turn an 'I can't' into an 'I can'.
- Help your child set specific goals they can achieve.
- Stop using personal negative language about them.

Real mum's advice

My daughter asked me to draw a kitten for her to colour. I said 'I'll have a go but a kitten is hard!'. 'Draw an easy kitten then' she said. I learn so much from her.

DAY 10: YOUR HEART CHART

Over the past few days, you've achieved a great deal in terms of focusing on being the parent you want to be. You'll already have started to notice a positive difference as you've started to focus and prioritise.

Today, focus on the symbol of the heart. It's extremely powerful. As a mum or a dad, you're at the very heart of your family.

Real mum's advice

I realised that my heart chart was full of words like 'smiling', 'fun', 'laughing'. But those things had gone out of my family life. I put my chart on the fridge as a reminder and now I really enjoy making sure we find time for family fun. I feel like a child myself again.

TOP TIP

- Find something to laugh about before breakfast every day. It'll get your day off to a great start.

Activity

Create your own heart chart

Draw a heart in the centre of a piece of paper. In the heart write 'I am'. Focus on what being the parent you want to be really means for you. Focus on the specific skills, qualities, feelings or activities you want to demonstrate.

Draw a line out from the heart and write one skill or quality that will finish the sentence 'I am'. Make sure you phrase everything positively. Instead of saying, for example, 'I don't want to lose my temper', say, 'I want to be calm and in control in challenging situations'.

Here's how one mum's heart chart looked. Now create your own.

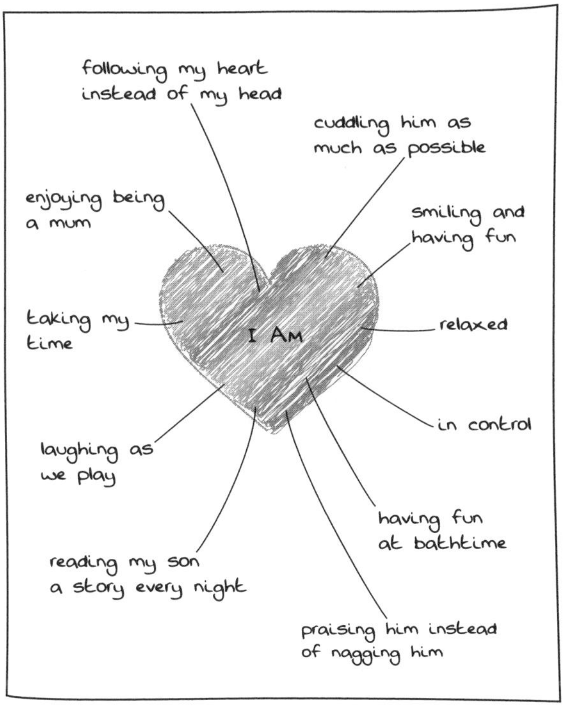

Your notes

CHAPTER 3

LOVE YOURSELF AND LOVE YOUR FAMILY

Today, our focus is on love. It's the greatest gift that you can give your child – and the greatest gift they can give to you.

Easy to love...

It's easy to love your baby when they smile at you, your toddler when they squeeze your hand, your eight-year-old when they give you that birthday card they made themselves that's covered in glue. Or your teenager when you hear them say to their mate that you're all right!

Hard to love...

It's much more difficult to love your child when they're being challenging, difficult or demanding. But that's the time when it's most important to love your child. Whatever their age, the time they most need your love is when it's the toughest to give.

TOP TIP

- When your child is at their most challenging, look at them and focus on what you love most about them. Don't see a devil – look for the angel in them.

Real mum's advice

At bedtime, we cuddle together and I tell my toddler what I've loved about being with her during the day. It's my favourite time of the day.

Activity

What do you love about your child?

You may often tell your child you love them. But how often do you talk to them specifically about *what it is* you love about them? Look into your child's eyes and focus on the three things you love most about them.

1. ....

....

2. ....

....

3. ....

....

Now tell them what you love about them – don't assume that they can read your mind. Get into the habit of doing this at least once a day. It's good for you – and it's great for them. Even a baby who can't understand your words yet will feel valued and secure – they'll sense the love in your voice.

Love is good for your heart

What do you love most about being a mum or a dad? It can be much easier to focus on the problems of parenthood instead of what you enjoy about it. That's human nature. But it's important that you do appreciate the positives – and get into the habit of celebrating what you love about being a parent. It will send a powerful message to your family. It will open your heart. It will boost your capacity to love and be loved.

See the big picture

What's more, the love you feel will help you to put any parental problems into perspective – and deal with them effectively rather than let them control you.

Real mum's advice

I have a 'memory box' full of cards and pictures that my children have made for me. It's my most precious possession. We all have so much fun looking through it and every picture brings back such wonderful memories.

Activity

Question time

Take a look at the following questions and record your answer to them on a tape recorder, CD or video – or write them down in a letter. Go with your gut instinct and say what you feel. Don't think about what the answer should be – talk from your heart.

1. What do you love most about being a parent?

2. What's your strongest memory of being a mum or dad – describe it.

3. How has being a parent helped you to grow in positive ways that you could never have imagined possible?

Keep your tape, CD or letter safe and play it or read it whenever you want to boost your X Factor and enjoy a little love energy.

TOP TIP

- Every year when it's your child's birthday, add another message to your tape, CD or letter. It'll be a living record of the amazing ways in which they've changed your life forever. Instead of buying an expensive 18th birthday present – give it to them. You won't be around forever – this will be a gift they'll always treasure.

If you're going to love your child to full capacity and with maximum impact, it's vital that you love, nurture and value yourself.

Recharge your batteries

If you're feeling good about yourself and positive about life, your children will benefit. If you're feeling tired and stressed, all of you will suffer. If you look after yourself, you're in a better position to look after your child. You're on call 24/7. Recharge those batteries – or you'll end up feeling like one of those rejected Christmas toys that's seen better days!

TOP TIP

- Create at least an hour of 'me' time at least once a week. Plan it in advance and make it happen.
- If you have a partner, talk to them and give each other 'time out'.
- Set up a support network of mums in the same boat and give each other a break.
- Book a babysitter you trust.

Real mum's advice

I found my mother-in-law difficult, but I asked her to babysit on a regular basis so that I could go for a swim. It's great. She loves looking after Charlie – and I find her much easier to get on with once I've had a bit of exercise and am feeling more positive.

Activity

Me time

Award yourself one point for each 'me time' activity you've enjoyed in the past week.

Me time	Score
• Took a peaceful bath	______
• Enjoyed a pampering treatment, e.g. massage, manicure	______
• Did an energy-boosting activity, e.g. walk, swim, gym	______
• Read a paper, magazine or book	______
• Had an evening out	______
• Drank a cup of tea without thinking about the housework	______
• Booked a babysitter	______
• Wore clothes I felt great in	______
• Did something new	______
• Went to bed feeling energised instead of shattered	______
Total score	______

Your score

0–4: You need to make big changes.
5–7: You're doing OK – but there's room for improvement.
8–10: Well done! You're investing time in yourself and everyone will benefit.

DAY 14: CELEBRATE YOUR STRENGTHS

What do you really think about yourself? As a parent, you're probably much more used to being self-critical than celebrating your strengths. We're great at giving ourselves a hard time and hopeless at patting ourselves on the back.

What limiting self-beliefs stop you enjoying being a mum or dad and getting the most out of family life? How often do you stop to think about the special skills and qualities that make you a great parent?

TOP TIP

- The more time you waste thinking about your negatives, the more negative you will feel.
- The more time you invest in focusing on your positives, the more positive you will feel.
- When you feel you're struggling as a parent, focus on the positive qualities that will help you cope with challenges.

Real dad's advice

I found it really hard to start the list, but once I got going I surprised myself. It made me feel good and I keep it in my wallet – just to remind myself.

Activity

What makes you a great parent?

Give yourself a maximum of three minutes to write down a list of things that make you a great parent. You may be breaking the habits of a lifetime, but focus only on positive attributes and keep your head clear of any negatives.

My challenge to you is to find ten positives. Come on – you can do it!

Ten good reasons that make me a great parent

1. ....

2. ....

3. ....

4. ....

5. ....

6. ....

7. ....

8. ....

9. ....

10. ....

It's time now to focus on what your child loves about having you as a mum or a dad. Being a parent is the most important role you'll ever play, and the love your children experience in their relationship with you will affect them for the rest of their lives.

With love, the stakes are high and the rewards are amazing.

Put yourself in their shoes

Get into the habit of putting yourself in their shoes. They may still be a baby in your arms or a hormonal teenager stretching you to the limit – but see yourself through their eyes. What is it about the way you are, or what you do or say, that helps them to feel loved, valued and secure? What is it about the way you are, or what you do or say, that boosts the love they feel for you?

TOP TIP

- In today's activity, be specific about the words you want to hear your child using.
- When you have filled your heart, put it somewhere really visible to remind you about the love you have in your life and all the joys that are to come. It's a constant reminder of the power of love.

Activity

Fill your love heart chart

Take a piece of A4 paper and draw a heart that fills the page.

Imagine that you're much older now and that your children are grown up with children of their own. As they look back on their childhood, what do you want to hear them saying about what they loved most about it – and what they love about having you as their mum or dad? This is your opportunity to write your own script – and make it happen. Enjoy.

Your notes

CHAPTER 4

TANTRUM-BUSTING TIPS

You know how it feels when your child has a tantrum – and you end up having one too. You begin to say and do things you wouldn't if you were calm. Your child is stamping their feet and shouting. You are too. You're acting their age instead of yours. You feel angry. You feel guilty. You feel sad.

The first step in dealing with children's tantrums is to tackle your own.

Fact

If you shout and stamp your feet to get your own way, that's what your child will learn to do too.

Activity

Deal with tantrums

Take a trip around your home and deal with tantrums – one room at a time. As you go into each room, focus on what you enjoy most and least about spending time in that room with your child. Which rooms do you feel best about – and which are the worst offenders?

Go back to the room in your home where you shout or get wound up more than any other. You may go bonkers in the bedroom. Or have bedlam in the bathroom. Perhaps meals are mayhem. Or the TV room is terrifying. Close your eyes and imagine you and your child are having fun there. Picture both of you giggling and laughing. Think specifically about the activity you're both enjoying. Paint the details of the picture in your mind.

TOP TIP

- Challenge your negative associations with the 'tantrum' room in your house. The next time you're in it with your child, make that great experience you visualised in today's activity into a reality for both of you. Change your view of that room – and start to change yourself. Make it happen today.

Real mum's advice

Bath times had become a real chore for me. It was loud and messy. I just wanted to get Tilly out as quickly as possible. I decided to have a bath with her. It was such fun – and loud and messy!

DAY 17: COMMIT TO CALMING DOWN

You may think that it's your child who sends you off the deep end and makes you lose your temper. You're not alone. Every child will throw tantrums and every parent knows what a nightmare it is. The answer lies with you – not your child. You can't force your child to behave, but you can change the way you respond to their tantrums and this will bring about changes in them.

You are the adult in this relationship. They're learning about life from you. If you're calm and in control when you deal with challenging situations, your child will be too.

'First keep the peace within yourself, then you can also bring peace to others.'
Thomas a Kempis (1380–1471), German mystic and religious author

Activity

Make it happen

Get out of your home and go for a walk around the block. Get some fresh air and commit to a fresh approach to dealing with tantrums. Focus on all the things you can do to help you keep calm and in control when your child is at their most demanding. It won't just happen. You'll make it happen.

TOP TIP

Dos

- Watch out for the warning signs before you have a full-blown tantrum and deal with them.
- Breathe deeply as you count to ten. Feel calmer as you focus on every breath.
- Decide in advance what you will do if your toddler throws a tantrum so you have a plan set up.

Don'ts

- Don't take anything they say or do personally. This is about them learning to be independent – it's not about you.
- Don't see a child being deliberately difficult – see the child you love.
- Don't let them control you. You're the adult so act your age – not theirs!

Real mum's advice

Believe in yourself. My two-year-old definitely had control in our house. But the day I started to believe that I could handle her tantrums well – was the day I did. We started playing by my rules – not hers.

Craving attention

Your child craves your attention. The most common reason that they will behave in a certain way is because they want you to notice them.

Your child wants your attention. Ideally, they'd like it to be good attention in the form of smiles, cuddles and praise. But failing that, any attention is better than no attention. So even when you're telling them off, you're giving them attention – and reinforcing the behaviour you're desperate to stop.

TOP TIP

- Follow this simple ABC.

  Acknowledge their good behaviour and ignore their bad behaviour.
  Boundaries need to be clear and positive.
  Consistency is essential or you're sending your child mixed messages.

Activity

Progress check

Complete the toddler-taming quiz to find out what you're doing well and what you need to work on. Think about what you've done this week and circle 'Yes' or 'No'. Score one point for every 'Yes'.

- Acted their age not yours — Yes/No
- Let your child have their own way because it was easier — Yes/No
- Spent more time telling them off than telling them what they did well — Yes/No
- Said 'no' more often than 'yes' — Yes/No
- Raised your voice to tell them to be quiet — Yes/No
- Made a promise you knew you were unlikely to keep – to make them behave — Yes/No
- Spent more time telling them what not to do – than what to do — Yes/No
- Made a threat to make them behave but didn't carry it out — Yes/No
- Bought them something you didn't really want to spend money on — Yes/No
- Let them watch more TV or play on the computer more than you wanted to — Yes/No

Total score ________

Your score

0–4: Good. You're definitely on the right road.
5–7: When you're feeling strong, you're performing well. Be more consistent.
8–10: Get a life and take control. You're making life difficult for yourself.

DAY 19: TOP TEN TANTRUMS

It can be hard if your child has a tantrum at home. But it can be even more stressful if they throw one in the supermarket, at the nursery or in a parent and toddler group. You can feel as though everyone's looking at you and thinking 'What a bad parent!' You're not alone. Parents who witness public tantrums will be sympathetic – not judgemental. They'll be feeling for you because they know exactly what you're going through.

Activity

Identify tantrum hotspots

Take a look at the list of ten tantrum hotspots and identify three useful tips for you to put into practice today.

DAY 19: TOP TEN TANTRUMS

Tantrum hotspot	Top tips
Supermarket trolley rage	• Shop at less busy times or online. • Avoid going when they're tired or hungry. • Have fun playing shopping 'eye spy'.
TV tantrums	• Avoid TV before meals or bedtime. • Spend time having fun without the TV. • Review your own TV habits.
Refusing meals	• Sit and eat with them. • Get them involved in preparing food. • Praise them for eating.
Car-seat chaos	• Loosen straps when you take them out. • Give them a special car toy only when they're strapped in. • Make sure other passengers wear seatbelts.
No to nursery	• Leave your home in plenty of time. • Talk to the nursery staff and tackle together. • Give yourself a day off and arrange for a friend to take them.
Refusing to go to bed	• Spend time in the bedroom having fun during the day. • Reduce daytime sleeping time. • Do at least one physical activity with them during the day.
Refusing to share toys	• Before other children arrive, put any favourite toys away. • Get out toys that are better to play with two children rather than one. • Praise your child for sharing.
Refusing to leave	• Give your child a ten-minute warning. • Leave time to make a game of clearing up. • Get them excited about what you're doing next.
Refusing to sit in the pushchair	• Encourage them to strap their toys into their toy buggy. • Be unpredictable – jump into the buggy and let them push you. • Play 'buggy' games.
Refusing to get dressed	• De-junk your child's wardrobe. • Encourage them to dress their toys. • Let them help to dress themselves.

DAY 20: YOUR TANTRUM STAR CHART

Star charts work well for children of all ages – and you can benefit as a parent too. They're a good way of encouraging and praising behaviour, for example, 'Cleared away toys', 'Did homework', 'Helped Dad with the washing up'. You're never too old to do a star chart. So have a go and see how it helps you. It'll also help you understand the benefits – and challenges – for your child.

Golden rules for successful star charts

1. Make them simple and specific.
2. Be consistent.
3. Put them somewhere very visible.
4. Decide what treat will be awarded on completion – this is good for motivation.
5. Involve your child in the process.

Activity

Make your own tantrum chart

Make your own tantrum-taming chart – for you and the way you behave. Put it somewhere where it's clearly visible. You can adapt it to suit your individual tantrum targets.

You have 24 hours. In this time, award yourself a sticker or draw a star or smiley face when you demonstrate the good behaviour. Your aim is to get one sticker in every box over the next day. Count your stickers and write down your score. Your maximum score will be ten – and that deserves a treat!

You can do it if you want to. Good luck!

DAY 20: YOUR TANTRUM STAR CHART

Parents' star chart

Your good behaviour	Achieved
Ignored their bad behaviour	
Praised their good behaviour	
Caught them 'red-handed' being good	
Acted your age – not theirs	
Created a boundary – and stuck to it	
Told yourself 'I can handle this well'	
Calmed down before speaking	
Told them what to do instead of what not to do	
Talked calmly instead of shouting	
Enjoyed the challenge of being a parent	
Marks out of 10	**/10**

Real mum's advice

I asked my two children to help me create my star chart and tell me what they wanted me to do. It was a real eye-opener as they both had 'stop shouting' at the top of their list. It made me focus and I made some real improvements.

Your notes

CHAPTER 5

CHILDREN UNPLUGGED – MAKE SURE *YOU* HAVE VOLUME CONTROL

DAY 21: ARE YOU A NOISY PARENT?

One of the greatest challenges for you as a parent is dealing with family noise. It's hard to think at times – let alone be heard above all the competition. The TV is on and your children are arguing. The washing machine's spinning and the phone rings. You shout 'Tea's ready' but no-one appears. You shout louder. Nothing. Suddenly you realise your home has no volume control.

But how noisy are you? Yes, I'm afraid that you're likely to be one of the main culprits when it comes to noise pollution in your own home.

TOP TIP

- Be honest with yourself. Most parents are surprised to find out just how noisy they are – they think it's just the children.

Real mum's advice

Get down to the same level as your child when you're talking to them. I found that really helped us both be a lot quieter.

Activity

Check out your noise levels

Read the following statements. Score one point for every 'Yes'.

- I have the radio on when I'm not listening to it. ________
- I have the TV on when I'm not watching it. ________
- I raise my voice so I can be heard over the noise of the TV or radio. ________
- I raise my voice so I can be heard over the noise of the children. ________
- I shout out to my children when they're in a different room. ________
- I only have the telephone answer machine on when I'm away from home. ________
- I have a mobile phone that's always switched on. ________
- I raise my voice to tell my children to stop being so noisy. ________
- I communicate more loudly than if I was talking to an adult. ________
- I raise my voice or shout more often than I want to. ________

Total score ________

Your score
0–3: You have good volume control.
4–7: Too loud. Turn it down!
8–10: There's serious work to do.

DAY 22: TURN DOWN YOUR VOLUME

Well, you can't unplug the children. But you can make sure you have volume control! Before you even start to deal with your children, it's time to get the volume zapper working on you.

You are your child's most powerful role model and they will take their lead from you. It's time for you to shape up and turn your volume down. If your normal noise levels are unacceptable – theirs will be too. You may not even have noticed that you've developed some undesirable habits.

Be honest with yourself

Be honest with yourself. Just by focusing on some of the key noisy parent areas, you're raising your awareness of just how noisy you are. These are all things you can change because you're in control of them. Take it one step at a time and you'll notice an immediate difference.

TOP TIP

- Keep working at it – it'll be worth it. You may be breaking habits developed over years.

Activity

Cut your noisy parent score

Here are three things you can do today that will cut your noisy parent score. If you achieve one of them, award yourself a bronze medal. If you achieve two, score silver. If you manage all of them, award yourself a gold medal.

- Only switch the TV or radio on if there is a specific programme you really want to watch or listen to – even when the children are in bed.
- Go into the room where your children are if you want to say something to them.
- Switch your answer machine on and your mobile off for at least one hour.

How did you do? Circle the appropriate word below.

I have successfully cut down my noise levels and am a bronze/silver/gold medallist!

Real dad's advice

I played a whispering game with my daughter. We were in a fairy kingdom and we both had to whisper. It made me realise just how loud I am normally – she's fine!

DAY 23: TV DETOX

The TV is likely to be the prime culprit when it comes to unacceptable noise levels in your home. For many, it's constantly on – even when nobody's watching. If you control the zapper, television can be a great source of entertainment. If you don't, it can be the enemy.

It's time for a serious TV detox in your home. If you treat the TV as an essential part of the family, it's likely your children will too. Focus today on just how important that box in the corner of the room has become in your family life and what influence it's having on you and your children.

TOP TIP

- Decide how much TV you're happy for your children to watch and stick to specific times.
- Know what they're watching. Watch a programme with them at least once a week – whether they're a toddler or teenager.
- Keep mealtimes a TV-free zone.

Real dad's advice

Don't be tempted to put the spare TV in their bedroom when you buy a new one. Give it to someone who'll really appreciate it.

'What bothers me about TV is that it tends to take our minds off our minds.' Robert Orban

Activity

Who's in charge of the remote?

Answer the following questions to find out who controls the TV zapper in your home. You? Or your children? Count up the number of As and Bs.

	A	B
Who watches most TV?	You	Your children
Who chooses what your children watch?	You	Your children
Is the TV a reason why things take longer, for example, getting dressed?	No	Yes
Do your children watch more TV than you want them to?	No	Yes
Do your children watch programmes you've never seen?	No	Yes
Do you give in to their demands to watch TV because its easier than arguing?	No	Yes
Do you let them watch the TV at the same time as eating?	No	Yes
Is there a TV in their bedroom?	No	Yes
Do you have TV house rules?	Yes	No
Total score		

Your score
Mostly As: You control the TV zapper.
Mostly Bs: Your children control your TV zapper.

By making a positive decision about when you want them to have the TV on, you're making a big difference in the family home. You've taken control of the TV zapper and are now playing by your rules not theirs.

Activity

Keep it quiet

Now it's time to help your children communicate at normal levels instead of raising their voices or shouting to be heard.

Catch them 'red-handed' being good! Of course, make sure that you don't ask them to do anything that you're not doing yourself.

Buy some stickers and award them one each time they demonstrate one of the following:

- switching the TV, games console or video off and doing something else instead
- talking quietly
- being in the same room as you when they talk to you
- waiting until someone else has finished talking before they begin
- listening without interrupting.

Ask them for their ideas too – they may surprise you. Explain to them exactly what the sticker is for and see how many they can accumulate during the day.

TOP TIP

- Explain to them what you want them to do instead of what you don't want them to do. This will always be much more effective. It will also help you to focus on achieving what you want to.

Do say
- Look at me when I'm talking so I can see your beautiful eyes.
- Talk quietly.
- I can hear what you're saying if you take it in turns.
- I'll listen if you talk to me.

Don't say – or shout!
- I know you're not listening – you're watching TV.
- Don't shout.
- I can't hear a thing if you're all shouting at once.
- I'm not doing anything if you shout.

Real dad's advice

Let them give you a sticker when you're being good too. They love it.

DAY 25: CREATE FAMILY TALK-TIME

By now you should be enjoying much lower levels of noise in your family home. Now's the day to enjoy making the most of it.

Two ears and one mouth

Ever wondered why you have two ears and only one mouth? It's so that you can listen to your children more than talk at them – and learn things you never even knew about them!

Identify one time today when you're going to really focus on listening to what your children have to say. It may be at a mealtime, when walking back from nursery or at bathtime. You decide when's a good time.

TOP TIP

- Sit down and talk to them.
- Give them your full attention – don't say you're listening when you're not.
- Switch off the TV and radio.
- Don't fill the dishwasher or unload the washing machine when you're chatting to them.
- Get into the habit of finding out something new about them every day.

Activity

How well do you know your child?

How well do you know your child? Have fun finding out. Have a look at the questions opposite and see what you think their answers would be. For the moment of truth, check them out with your child when you're enjoying family talk-time and see how well you know them.

	Your answer	Their answer
What do they like most about living in your house?		
Who's their best friend/ favourite teacher?		
What do they want to be when they grow up?		
What's their favourite TV programme		
What's their favourite food?		
What's their favourite drink?		
What's their favourite way to travel? Car? Plane? Train? Bus? Walking? Scooter?		
What's their favourite colour?		
What do they most enjoy playing with you?		
What story is their favourite for you to read to them at bedtime?		
Total score		

Your score
1–4 matched answers: Come on. Get listening.
5–8 matched answers: Good. Keep going.
9–10 matched answers: Excellent. You invest time in getting to know them.

'When people talk, listen completely. Most people never listen.'
Ernest Hemingway (1899–1961), US writer

Your notes

CHAPTER 6

ROUTINES OR RUTS?

By the end of each day of our journey so far, you've taken one step closer to becoming the parent you want to be – from screamer to sweet dreamer.

After completing the activities so far in this book, you may already have made important changes to your bedtime routines. The next few days are an opportunity to set up a routine that you're happy with. Alternatively, raise your game and transform your evening routines from OK to great.

The importance of routines

Routines are absolutely essential for you and your child. They're liberating – not restricting.

Activity

How good are your and your child's routines?

Take a look at the following statements.

Score 3 points if you're strong in this area, 2 if you're average and 1 if it's a definite no-no.

	Score
• I have a relaxing bedtime routine that works.	________
• I enjoy spending time in my bedroom.	________
• My bedroom is my sanctuary with no junk and no toys.	________
• I have enough energy in the evening to do something for me that I enjoy.	________

	Score
• My child has a bedtime routine that works for them.	________
• I know specifically what I want my child's evening routine to be.	________
• I control what happens in our home in the evenings – not my child.	________
• I go to bed feeling positive about what I have achieved in the day.	________
• I go to bed looking forward to what the next day will bring.	________
• I only watch the TV programmes I really want to watch.	________
Total score	________

Your score

0–9: You're more likely to have nightmares than sweet dreams!

10–20: You're an occasional sweet dreamer – work at it.

21–30: Congratulations, sweet dreamer.

The starting point is you.

A relaxing routine is just as important for you as it is for your child. Yes, there may be the occasions when you choose to break it – but the routine's there and it's just as you want it.

If you have a relaxing evening routine, and go to sleep with positive thoughts, you'll feel much more motivated and constructive.

Five good reasons to have a relaxing routine

- You'll be motivated to tackle any bedtime challenges you have with your child.
- You'll be more relaxed with your child.
- You'll sleep better and have more energy to be the parent you want to be.
- You'll look forward to evenings – not dread them.
- You deserve it.

Activity

Plan your ideal evening

Write down your *ideal* evening schedule – not just the one that happens now. If you don't have an ideal to aim for, you're unlikely to get close to it.

Start your schedule from the time your children are in bed. Break the evening down into ten-minute segments and make a note of what *you want* to be doing at that time. Be specific and positive.

Now you have your schedule, make it happen. Do one thing each evening that will help take you one step closer to having the evening you want.

TOP TIP

- If you have a partner, talk to them about sharing putting your child to bed so that both of you get a chance to relax.
- Enjoy a luxurious bubble bath or pamper yourself.
- Find yourself a good magazine or book that you'll look forward to reading.
- Use scented candles to create a relaxing bedroom environment.

Real mum's advice

I used to climb into bed exhausted. I'd put the TV on because I was too tired to do anything and I'd fall asleep with it on full blast. I took the TV out of my room and found myself a good book to read instead. I really look forward to reading it before I go to sleep now.

'There is always a moment in childhood when the door opens and lets the future in.' Graham Green, author

DAY 28: THEIR GOOD-NIGHT ROUTINES

Many parents find that it's their children who control their bedtime routines – they play by their children's rules and not by their own. The key to establishing a good evening routine and sweet dreams for your child is:

S Specific schedules
W Want to make it happen
E Enjoy the challenge
E Encourage your child to be active during the day
T Try something new

D Decide you'll stick to your routine for three consecutive days
R Recognise that short-term pain brings long-term gain
E Equip yourself with advice from experts
A Always be consistent – even when it's tough
M Motivate using praise and sticker charts
S Step by step you will achieve success

Five good reasons for your child to have a bedtime routine

- They'll feel secure and know what to expect.
- They'll look forward to spending positive time with you.
- They'll get a good night's sleep.
- They'll feel more energetic in the morning.
- They deserve it.

Activity

Plan your child's routine

Write down your *ideal* evening schedule for them. Break the evening down into ten-minute segments and write what you want to be doing at that time. Be specific and positive. On a scale of 1 to 10, how close are you to achieving that ideal schedule? A score of 10 out of 10 shows that you're achieving it. A score of 1 out of 10 indicates that there's a long way to go.

1	2	3	4	5	6	7	8	9	10

Now you have your schedule, make it happen. Do one thing each evening that will help take you one step closer to having the evening you want.

TOP TIP

- Trust your gut instinct.
- Place a regular order for a parenting magazine like *Practical Parenting* to support you with your everyday challenges.
- Read Parentalk's *Guide To Sleep* by Kate Daymond (available at www.parentalk.co.uk)
- Ask your health visitor about local sleep clinics.

The evening can be the most challenging time for parents and for children. You may not have seen your children because you've been out at work. But you're tired after a demanding day. They're tired too.

It can be the time when stress levels are high and patience is low. Bedtime can develop into a full-blown war. But no matter how tense you feel or what you've said or done, always deal with it before you get into bed. If you don't it will fester and grow. You'll feel angry and guilty and sad and negative.

Activity

Remind yourself of the good bits

Choose a sweet note or card or picture that your child has sent to you. Put it in a place where it's easily seen by their bed so that it's a constant reminder of your special relationship. Any time you feel challenged at bedtime – take a quick look to remind you just how lovely they are. It'll help you feel much more positive and in control.

TOP TIP

- Every time you feel challenged by your child, say this to yourself: 'I love (their name) and I want them to know that I love them and am always here for them.'
- Don't go to sleep with negative thoughts – always go to sleep with positive ones. If there is a bridge to be built, you start building it... don't wait for them.

Real mum's advice

I always have a cuddle with Tom and tell him what I love about being his mum. The other evening I was so cross with him that I didn't do it. But he took the wind out of my sails by saying 'I still love you mum – even when you shout.'

DAY 30: I'M MOVING FORWARD

It's time to see just how far you've come with this since the beginning of the chapter. You have:

- set yourself specific goals for you and your child
- established routines and communicated them clearly
- committed to make positive changes.

TOP TIP

- Treat yourself to celebrate any positive progress that you have made since the beginning of this chapter.

Real mum's advice

I teamed up with another mum who was having problems getting her toddler to sleep through the night and we supported each other. It was great to be sharing the challenge with someone who knew what you were going through. We both cracked it.

Activity

Take a look at the following statements.

Score 3 if you've made a significant step forward in this area, 2 if you've moved forward a little and 1 if you've stayed in the same place.

	Score
• I have a relaxing bedtime routine that works.	________
• I enjoy spending time in my bedroom.	________
• My bedroom is my sanctuary with no junk and no toys.	________
• I have enough energy in the evening to do something for me that I enjoy.	________
• My child has a bedtime routine that works for them.	________
• I know specifically what I want my child's evening routine to be.	________
• I control what happens in our home in the evenings – not my child.	________
• I go to bed feeling positive about what I have achieved in the day.	________
• I go to bed looking forward to what the next day will bring	________
• I only watch the TV programmes I really want to watch.	________
Total score	________

Your score

0–9: The person holding you back is you.
10–20: Good. Take it a step at a time.
21–30: Congratulations – you're making great changes.

Your notes

CHAPTER 7

GOOD OR GUILTY? BE YOUR OWN JUDGE

DAY 31: TAKE YOURSELF OUT OF THE DOCK

Guilt is a very powerful negative word. It's a word that can have a profound effect on the way you feel about yourself as a parent and on your family life. If you let it, it can become a weapon of mass destruction that you use on yourself.

Guilt is a strong emotive word. You usually hear it in the courts when people are accused of criminal activity – not in everyday life. Many parents – especially mums – put themselves in the dock and say they feel guilty. What's more, they'll usually say that it's a word they rarely used about themselves before they had children – perhaps occasionally if they treated themselves to a chocolate or piece of cake! Now they use it on a regular basis.

TOP TIP

- Today is the day to stop *wasting* time feeling guilty. The process of feeling guilty doesn't help you at all – it just makes you feel worse. *Invest* time instead in positive actions that will help you feel good, not make you feel guilty about being a parent. Both you and your child will benefit. Take control – and wave goodbye to your guilt gremlin!

Activity

How guilty do you feel?

Take a look at the top ten guilt hotspots and see how many of them affect you.

Top ten guilt hotspots

- You feel guilty about being away from your child.
- You feel guilty about having to say 'no' to your child.
- You feel guilty about stopping breastfeeding.
- You feel guilty about shouting at your child.
- You feel guilty about being negative with your child.
- You feel guilty about being too tired to be a fun parent.
- You feel guilty about childcare.
- You feel guilty about leaving work on time when colleagues stay.
- You feel guilty about not enjoying being a mum all the time.
- You feel guilty about having any 'me' time.

Total score __________

Your score

0–3: You're feeling good.
4–7: Be careful – your guilt gremlin has a hold on you.
8–10: Your guilt gremlin's taken control of your life!

Mums and dads are good at making themselves feel guilty – and not so good at letting themselves feel good. They give themselves a very hard time.

The negative influence of guilt

The bad news about guilt is that it can have a very powerful negative impact on your life – if you let it. The good news is that you're in control of the way you feel. You can change the way you respond to situations and reduce how guilty you feel. That leaves you with less stress and more energy – so that you can get on and enjoy being a mum.

It's time to give your guilt gremlin a sleepless night – instead of it doing that to you!

TOP TIP

- Every time your guilt gremlin rears its ugly head, focus on all of the reasons you have to feel good – not guilty – about being a parent.
- We have an unhealthy tendency to focus on the negative – what we don't do, should have done or could do better. A positive approach is a healthy approach.

Real mum's advice

I always had a gremlin on my shoulder giving me plenty – especially when I was feeling tired. I decided to give him a name and every time he popped up, I'd say, 'Go away, Henry!' I got strange looks – but it really worked.

Activity

Five ways to get rid of your guilt gremlin

Focus on the negative effect your guilt gremlin has on you and your family.

It's important to take action today. The longer you let it hang around, the more powerful it'll become.

1 Draw a picture of it. Now tear it up and put it in the bin.

2 Imagine a picture of it in your mind and now gradually rub it out.

3 Cuddle your child and focus on what you do well as a parent.

4 Cuddle your child and focus on what they love about you.

5 Say, 'I feel good about being a parent' out loud to yourself – and believe it.

DAY 33: BE POSITIVE ABOUT CHILDCARE

The most common reason that mums give for feeling guilty is that they're struggling with the stressful challenge of combining a family with a career – and feel they're failing at both.

Feeling guilty about not being with your child is natural, so try not to be too hard on yourself. Juggling family and work is a huge challenge, especially when you're doing it for the first time. You love your child and you're feeling stressed about leaving them because you're passionate about being the best mum possible – and that's something to feel good about.

TOP TIP

- Find some really happy photos of your child laughing and smiling. Put those photos around you all the time – on your desk, on the fridge, on your mouse mat and in your handbag. When you think about your child, picture them laughing and having fun.

Real mum's advice

I got Freya to draw a picture showing her and her friends at nursery. It was great fun doing it and now I have it on the wall at work. I can look at it and know that she's having a good time with them.

Activity

Focus on the positives

Don't let your imagination run riot by convincing yourself that your child is unhappy because you're not with them. You've chosen a good childcare option and you're leaving your child with someone you like and trust.

Do

- Think about the activities your child enjoys most at nursery, etc. – picture them.
- Recognise the benefits that your child has from spending time with other adults and children.
- Enjoy being a mum. When you're with your child be the happiest parent – be 100 per cent mum!

Don't

- Don't say, 'I'll miss you' when you drop them off – say you're looking forward to seeing them later.
- Don't make the journey to and from the nursery or childminder a guilt trip – make it fun!
- Don't focus on what your child is missing out on by being at nursery.

DAY 34: TOP TEN GUILT-BUSTING IDEAS

The way you deal with your guilt is down to you. Instead of just letting it take a grip, make a positive and conscious effort to reduce its power over you.

Activity

Banish that guilt!

The more you talk about feeling guilty, the worse you'll feel. Challenge yourself to get through the day feeling good, not guilty and use some of our top ten guilt-busting tips to help.

1 **Stop using the word 'guilty'.** Talk about what makes you feel good about being a mum instead. Encourage other parents to do the same.

2 **Boost your energy.** Guilt thrives in parents who are tired and feeling vulnerable. Boost your healthy eating habits.

3 **Make play dates.** Set yourself a specific goal for your time with your child each week. Focus on what you do rather than what you don't do.

4 **Switch your mobile off.** When you're spending time with your children, switch it off. Don't be on call 24/7.

5 **Don't make false promises.** Say what you mean and mean what you say – you won't feel guilty about breaking your 'promises'.

6 **Spoil them with time not money.** Find five minutes to play with them instead of spending £5 on a toy for them.

7 **Enjoy guilt-free sleep.** Go to bed focusing on what's gone well during the day and what personal qualities have helped you to make this happen.

8 **Be 100 per cent a parent at home.** Stay away from your computer. Switch on the answer phone. Leave work at work.

9 **Talk to your child.** Talk to them about your positive feelings about being a parent.

10 **Make the most of bedtimes.** Give them a cuddle and tell them specifically what you love about being their mum or dad.

One of the big challenges that parents – especially mums – who go out to work face is that they feel guilty when they leave the office and their colleagues are still looking busy at their desks.

You've done a really good day's work and achieved a lot – but you still feel guilty about leaving the office on time to go and pick up your little one from the nursery or childminder.

Real dad's advice

I joined a support network for other parents at work. It's really helped. We can talk about the things we're struggling with that you wouldn't talk about in the pub.

'If you want to work for world peace, go home and love your families.' Mother Theresa

Activity

Try out the guilt-busting plan

Put this simple and effective guilt-busting plan into action today.

1. Spend your last five minutes at work writing down what you've achieved – instead of your 'to do' list for the next day.
2. Keep a record of that list to remind you of your achievements for your next review.
3. Read it to yourself and acknowledge that you've done a good job.
4. Commit to leave work at work and be 100 per cent mum or dad at home.
5. Leave work on time.
6. Enjoy knowing that employees are usually more focused, creative and productive once they have a family. You achieve more – not less.
7. Hold your head high and stand tall and straight. This is a positive action – don't try to slip out unnoticed.
8. Feel good, not guilty as you walk out through the door. Instead of focusing on the good reasons to stay at work, focus on the excellent reasons to leave.
9. Imagine your colleagues are surfing the net or playing chess against the computer instead of finishing off that board report – they may be.
10. Don't put it off until tomorrow – do it today.

Your notes

CHAPTER 8

BUILDING A FAMILY TEAM

DAY 36: WHAT KIND OF A FAMILY LEADER ARE YOU?

Building a family team is one of the most rewarding and challenging things you'll ever attempt to do as a parent. It's also absolutely vital if you want to achieve the best for your family.

As a family leader, you have great power – and with that comes great responsibility.

Five great reasons to build a family team

- You're helping your family develop important life skills.
- You're a powerful role model in resolving conflict.
- You're helping your family achieve their goals.
- You'll have more time and energy to enjoy being a parent.
- You're nurturing special qualities and talents in each individual.

TOP TIP

- Be completely honest. A great parent can learn as much from their weaknesses as they can from their strengths.

Real mum's advice

Every time you're tempted to do something yourself just because it's quicker – stop. You know you're only making a rod for your own back.

Activity

What kind of a family leader are you?

Read each of the statements below. Score 2 points if you're strong in that area, 1 if you're average and 0 points if there's lots of room for improvement.

	Score
• I have a vision for my family's future.	______
• I set regular family goals and achieve them.	______
• I encourage my family to talk about their feelings.	______
• We have regular family meetings.	______
• I praise myself/partner/child on a regular basis.	______
• I'm good at delegating.	______
• I provide new opportunities to help individuals develop.	______
• I resolve family conflict fairly and calmly.	______
• I'm willing to admit if I've made a mistake.	______
• I'm a good motivator.	______
Total score	______

Your score
0–9: There's lots of work to do.
10–15: There's great family leadership potential.
16–20: You're a skilled family team leader.

DAY 37: WHAT DO THE REST OF THE TEAM FEEL?

It's sometimes the case that the kind of team leader you think you are is quite different from how the rest of the family sees you. As an effective leader, it's useful and constructive to take on board how other people view your leadership as this will help you identify areas to improve.

TOP TIP

- Don't be defensive. Feedback from people you love and trust is always helpful – even when it's hard to take.
- Ask them to tell you what you're best at from today's list and the one area they'd like you to work on.

Real mum's advice

Listen and learn. My seven-year-old daughter told me I was always siding with her younger brother in arguments. She was right. I was softer on him because he's younger. Being fair is a priority for me now.

'A mother is not a person to lean on but a person to make leaning unnecessary.' Dorothy Canfield Fisher (1879–1958), American writer

Activity

How does your family rate you?

Ask your partner if you have one, your child (if they're old enough) or someone you trust to score you in the areas listed below. This will give you a fuller picture of the kind of family leader you are.

Ask them to read each of the statements and score 2 points if you're strong in that area, 1 point if you're average and 0 points if there's lots of room for improvement.

	Score
• I have a vision for my family's future.	________
• I set regular family goals and achieve them.	________
• I encourage my family to talk about their feelings.	________
• We have regular family meetings.	________
• I praise myself/partner/child on a regular basis.	________
• I'm good at delegating.	________
• I provide new opportunities to help individuals develop.	________
• I resolve family conflict fairly and calmly.	________
• I'm willing to admit if I've made a mistake.	________
• I'm a good motivator.	________
Total score	________

Take a look and see how your child or partner's ratings compare with yours (yesterday's task).

DAY 38: BUILDING YOUR FAMILY PYRAMID

All members of a team support each other. They have different qualities, experiences and skills. Your family is made up of brilliant and different individuals. Together, they're even stronger and amazing. This is your family – and you've every right to be proud of them.

The more you support each other, the stronger your family will be. It's often at times of crisis that we pull together as a family and find great comfort in the support we get from each other. As a great family leader, this is the kind of support you want to be inspiring and building in your family on a daily basis so that it's the rule – not the exception. We all need love and support if we're to flourish and grow.

TOP TIP

- Tell each child what special attributes and qualities they bring to the family team.

Real dad's advice

I asked my son – who is football mad – what player I reminded him of. 'I think you're nearly as good as David Beckham,' he said. It made me determined to raise my game and be a real team captain.

Activity

Where do you fit in your family pyramid?

Think of your family as a pyramid. If you're at the bottom, supporting all the members of your family without support yourself, your family is in a very weak position. It only needs a little something to upset your family equilibrium.

But if you're at the top of the pyramid, supported by all members of your family, you're in a very strong position.

Take a look at the two pyramids. Are you at the bottom holding everyone else up? Or are you at the top enjoying everyone's support? Which one best represents the role you play in your family?

DAY 39: BE AT THE HEART OF YOUR FAMILY

Building support in your family team will help you all in your daily lives and will put you in a particularly strong position when you're faced with a family crisis.

Boosting your family team

- Encourage your family to support each other.
- Be a positive and creative role model.
- Get everyone talking.
- Encourage a selfless instead of selfish approach to life.
- Talk about the benefits for the family as a whole.

Teaching the family team these skills will be useful not just within the family – but in every situation you all find yourselves in as you journey through life.

TOP TIP

- Use today's heart chart to encourage you – and your partner if you have one – to support each other. It can get you talking and provides a way to articulate practical ways to help each other – rather than shutting down!

Activity

Create your child's heart chart

This will help you to focus on specific ways of increasing the support you give to your family. Identify an issue where your child would benefit from your support. It can be anything – concerns about nursery, confidence, eating, being clingy or anxious, sibling rivalry, etc.

Draw a heart and put their name inside, together with the issue you want to focus on.

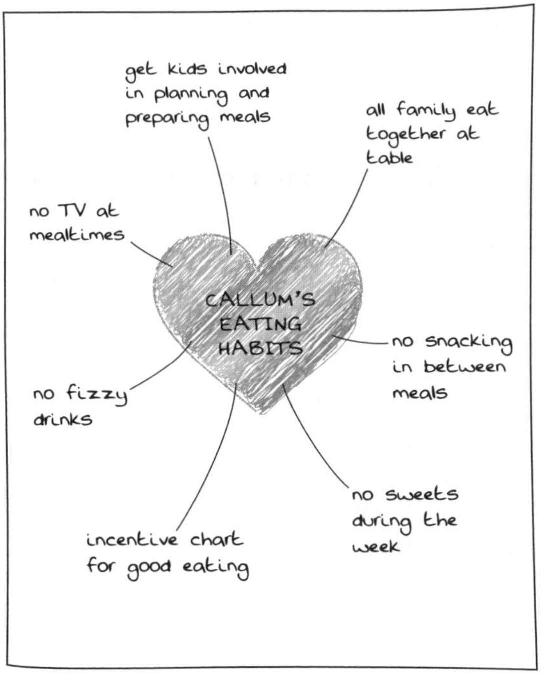

Now brainstorm ideas. Think of all the different ways that you can help to support your child with this issue – and encourage other family members to contribute too.

DAY 40: EFFECTIVE TEAM MEETINGS

An effective team leader holds regular family team meetings. Good communication is key to smooth family life, and you're teaching your child that discussion is always more effective than shouting. It's when communication breaks down that tantrums begin.

Five skills your child will develop

1. The ability to listen
2. The ability to respect different points of view
3. Effective conflict resolution
4. Strong communication skills
5. Leadership qualities

Dos and don'ts

Do

- Always include at least one fun item on the agenda – for example, a family outing, holiday, etc.
- Meet regularly.
- Live your values and treat them with respect – even in a one-way street!
- Give everyone the opportunity to talk without interruption.
- Motivate your team.
- Give clear and positive feedback.
- Set targets for the week.
- Do be calm and relaxed.
- Use positive language and open questions (these give them a chance to explain, rather than answering just 'yes' or 'no').

Don't

- Don't lose your cool.
- Don't cancel the meeting because it's easy too. It's the most important date in your family diary.
- Don't tell them what you're going to do.
- Don't turn it into a regular telling-off session.
- Don't threaten.

- Don't ask closed questions – those that can only have a 'yes' or 'no' answer.
- Don't take personal remarks – keep objective.
- Don't get defensive – or they will too.

Activity

Create an ideas box

Call your first family meeting. Create an ideas box so that all members of the family can put in things they want to discuss at the family meeting.

TOP TIP

- You will, of course, need to set boundaries for your children. But team meetings give you a chance to involve them in the process of establishing those boundaries. This is an opportunity for you to explain your feelings to them. It will also help them to understand that you don't want to lay down the law and make their life difficult – it's because you care for them.

Real mum's advice

My life was chaos with four children under nine years old. I asked my children to think of one thing they could each do to help me feel less stressed in the mornings. They came up with great ideas!

Your notes

CHAPTER 9

MOTIVATE AND BE MOTIVATED

The ability to motivate is one of your most precious assets as a parent. Motivated families are positive and energised. De-motivated families are negative and stressed.

Five good reasons to motivate

- You'll have more fun.
- You start seeing immediate results.
- You're teaching your child to motivate.
- You're tuning in to what really makes your child tick.
- You'll create a positive family life for everyone.

TOP TIP

- Focus on you. In order to succeed in motivating your child, you'll first need a good understanding of what motivates and de-motivates you. You'll know yourself just how good you feel when you're motivated and how it can help you find the energy and creativity to make things happen.

'Those who are going nowhere usually ger there.' Henry Ford, founder of the Ford Motor Company

Activity

How effective are you as a motivator?

Take a look at the statements below. Score 3 points if you're strong in that area, 2 points if you're OK in that area, and 1 point if there's lots of room for improvement.

	Score
• I'm good at achieving my goals.	______
• I'm good at setting specific goals for my child that they achieve.	______
• I usually tell my child what I want them to do rather than what I don't want to do.	______
• I'm consistent in praising my child.	______
• I'm good at making my child feel valued.	______
• I'm successful at ignoring my child's bad behaviour.	______
• I understand what makes my child tick.	______
• I'm successful at using alternatives to threats.	______
• I encourage my child to talk about their positive feelings.	______
• I'm creative in finding ways to motivate my child.	______
Total score	______

Your score
10–15: There are lots of areas to work on.
16–25: You perform well in key areas.
26–30: You're an excellent motivator.

Pain or gain?

Generally, parents use two kinds of motivational styles with their children.

The 'away from pain' parenting style

You try to get your child to behave in a certain way in order to avoid 'pain'. For example, 'If you don't stop arguing, I'll switch off the TV.' This style:

- ◆ involves 'pain' on the part of the children through the removal of treats or privileges
- ◆ involves threats and ultimatums
- ◆ uses negative language
- ◆ *discourages* certain behaviour – you tell them what *not to do*
- ◆ isn't enjoyable – you don't like being a 'pain' parent
- ◆ de-motivates.

The 'towards gain' parenting style

You try to get your child to behave in a certain way by providing a 'gain' or incentive. For example, 'When you're sitting together quietly, you can watch TV.' This style:

- ◆ involves 'gain' on the part of the children through praise, treats or privileges
- ◆ involves incentives
- ◆ uses positive language
- ◆ *encourages* a certain behaviour – you tell them what *to do*
- ◆ makes you feel good – you enjoy being a 'gain' parent
- ◆ motivates.

Activity

Tune into your parenting style

Over the next 24 hours, 'tune in' to your parenting style and really focus on the way you try to get your child to do something. By doing this, you'll discover if you're more of an 'away from pain' or 'towards gain' parent.

TOP TIP

- Don't be put off if you're much more of a 'pain' parent than you realised – many parents are. It's a habit you can easily slip into.
- Focus on being more gain and less pain from now on – if that's what you want to do.

Real mum's advice

I was much more negative than I thought I was. I wrote down the negative words I kept using again and again and again on my hand – and looked at it every time I talked to them to remind me to be positive instead.

DAY 43: TURN A 'NEED TO' INTO A 'WANT TO'

There's a big difference between what you feel you *need to do* – and what you *want to do*. If you're doing something you want to do, you're much more likely to be powerfully motivated to achieve it. If you're doing something you feel you need to do, you are likely to feel less motivated to achieve it.

Needs

If you need to do something, it will drain your energy. You're likely to find all sorts of reasons why you can't make it happen.

Wants

If you want to do it, you'll feel energised. You'll find reasons to make it happen.

TOP TIP

- Every time you're faced with a task that you don't want to do – think about how you can turn that 'need to' into a 'want to'.

Real dad's advice

I was always finding excuses not to re-decorate my son's bedroom. I started to imagine the smile I'd see on his face when he finally had his dream 'football bedroom'. It made me really want to do it.

Activity

What's your motivation?

Think about what motivates you to read this book. You're a busy parent. You've got lots of demands on your time and good reasons to do other things instead of this. On a scale of 1–10, how motivated do you feel about investing the time and energy to reach your destination? A score of 10 out of 10 indicates excellent motivation. A score of 1 out of 10 indicates low motivation.

Your score ____________

Motivation score of 8+
You have strong motivation. You *want* to complete this journey. You'll be successful at becoming the parent you *want* to be.

Motivation score of 7 or below
You have low motivation. You feel you need to complete this journey. You may be successful but it's not guaranteed.

Traffic lights and star charts

Star and sticker charts can be extremely effective motivational tools.

On your marks ...

Create your own traffic light using green, red and yellow A4 paper. Put your traffic light in a place where it's really visible. Write each child's name on a postcard or coloured sticker. Every child starts off on the green card (use Blu-tack or Velcro to attach).

Get set ...

The goal is for your child to complete the day/week and end up on the green square. Decide what you want the incentive to be. It may be praise – it may be a privilege or a treat.

Go!

This is how it works. When your child behaves in a way that's unacceptable to you or breaks a family rule, move them from the green to the yellow.

Once on yellow, they can return to the green if they do something that you can praise or that supports a family rule.

But, if they do something else that you want to discourage, move them onto the red. Once on the red, they can still move back through to yellow and green by behaving well.

Activity

Create your own traffic light system

Create your own traffic light system. Put it somewhere visible. Adapt it to suit your child. If they're really into football, call the green card the pitch, the yellow card a warning and the red card a send off. Use language they understand and motivate them to stay on the pitch.

Reasons parents stop using star and sticker charts

- They become too complicated to manage.
- They run out of stickers/paper and don't replace them.
- Parents can't remember why – they just did.

Real mum's advice

I was having real problems with my daughter arguing with my son. The traffic lights made getting on fun and they had to work together to stay on the green.

DAY 45: SCREEN TIME NOT SCREAM TIME!

The TV, computer and games console have turned screens into a focal point for many families. As a parent, you may start off feeling in control and enjoying the pleasure your child gets from them. Then one day you wake up and realise that they're out of control and the machines are having much more influence in your child's life than you want them to.

Welcome to the average family home!

Screen time

Lots of parents find that using 'screen time' as an incentive – instead of something that is always available – is helpful. Screen time means allocating a certain amount of time that your child can be on screen.

- It motivates you and your child.
- It means you take a hard look at what's going on in your home now.
- You can set the boundaries and control your child's screen time.
- You can be specific about what you want them to do in that screen time.
- You can use it to support learning.
- It becomes an incentive instead of a given.

Activity

Focus on your child's screen time

Write down how much screen time your child has today. Be specific about whether it's on the TV, computer, games console, etc.

Write down how much screen time you want them to have and when you want them to have it. How much of a gap is there between reality and your ideal?

Sit down with your child and draw up a motivational plan – set them a fun challenge so that they can earn screen time.

TOP TIP

- Involve your child in the motivation-making process.
- Use only positive language.
- Be specific about what exactly must be achieved and how much screen time this will earn them.
- Be calm and consistent.

Real mum's advice

My son said he wanted to play me at his favourite game as his treat. It was the first time I'd ever tried. We both had such a laugh!

Your notes

CHAPTER 10

SUCCESSFUL STRESS MANAGEMENT

DAY 46: STRESS MOT

The next step on our journey together is for you to begin to develop successful stress management strategies. There may be certain challenging aspects of your life or people who make your life difficult. There may be things that you can't control that cause you high levels of stress in your life. But there are certain things you can control, and one of these is the way you respond to challenges.

If things aren't quite going according to plan, it can be the children who take the brunt of the pressure we're feeling.

How do you handle stress?

Today we're going to focus on the way you handle the stresses and pressures of family life. If you want to manage your stress levels, it's important to focus on the specific aspects of your life that are causing it. Rather than thinking, 'I feel stressed about life', it's essential to break down the big 'life' picture into manageable chunks so that you can do something specific to reduce your stress levels.

> **Real dad's advice**
>
> I thought that the relationship with my toddler was going to be the most stressful area but I realise now that I'm doing quite well with that! It's my job that I need to change!

'Stress is an ignorant state. It believes that everything is an emergency. Nothing is that important.' Natalie Goldberg, writer

Activity

The parent wheel

Take a look at the circle below. Each segment represents an area of your life – one part of the big picture. The way you feel about each of the areas will affect the way you feel about being a parent. The words may mean different things to different people. Focus on one segment at a time and the stress you feel in that particular area of your life.

Which is the most stressful area of your life?

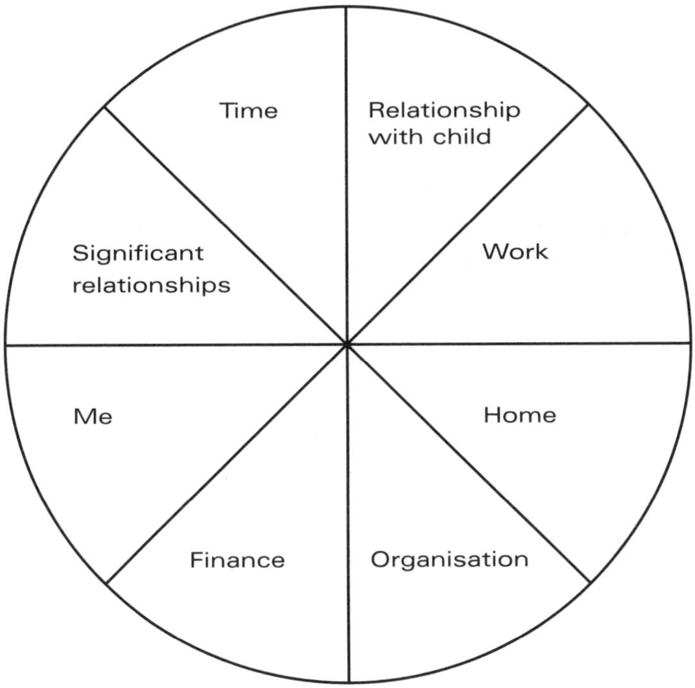

Steps to manage stress

There are just two steps you need to take in order to manage your stress successfully.

Step 1: Think positive

Spending time feeling stressed does nothing at all to help you deal with the stress. It just makes you feel worse. When you're stressed you're not living, you're existing. Your imagination runs wild. You feel isolated. You stand still. You need to start thinking positively in order to change things.

Step 2: Take action

If you keep on doing what you're doing, you'll keep on getting what you're getting. If you want to feel less stressed you have *to do* something differently. Instead of standing still, take action – one step at a time – and move forward.

TOP TIP

- Get into the habit of talking to your children about what they do well in different areas and help them build a positive life picture.
- When they face a challenge, help them break it down into manageable chunks.

Activity

Focus on your achievements

Yesterday, you focused on the parent wheel and identified a particular area of your life that was stressful for you.

Before you decide what to do, start with some positive thinking. If you want to deal with stress, create the optimum frame of mind to do it.

Take a look at the parent wheel again. This time, as you focus on each segment, think about what you are achieving in that area. Clear your mind of stresses and strains and think about what you do well. Identify one positive achievement in each part.

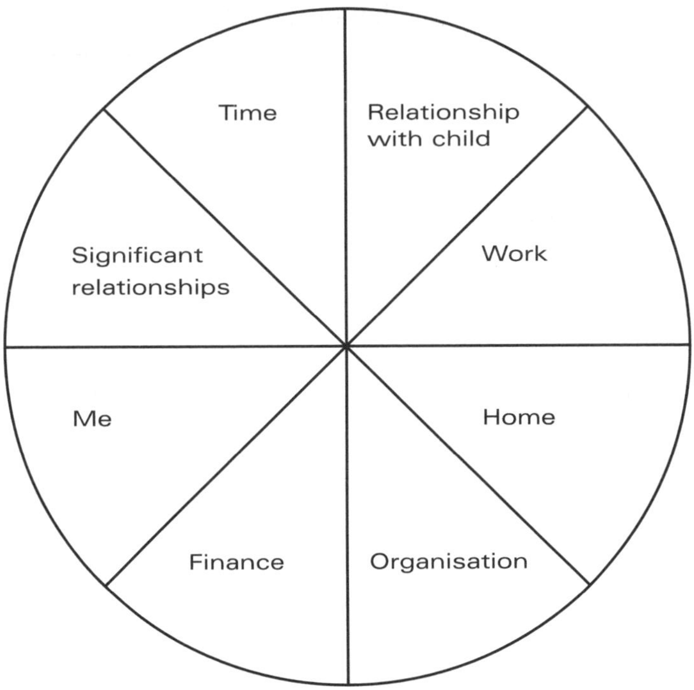

There may be stresses in one area of your life, but spend a couple of minutes thinking about your biggest achievement in that part of the wheel.

DAY 48: TAKE ACTION

Identify one practical thing that you could do today that would help you to feel more relaxed and less stressed about the area of your life we have now identified. Remember that it needs to be something *you* can do that is within *your control* and not dependent on anyone else.

Having choices to make in life may seem stressful, but once you make a decision about what you want to do, you'll reduce your stress levels. Not making a decision is always much more stressful than making a decision.

TOP TIP

- Make climbing the stress-free ladder easy for yourself – not difficult. Think of small, simple practical things you can do that will make a big difference.

Real mum's advice

Learn to relax. I took up Pilates. It was great. I decided to sign up for ten sessions instead of paying weekly so I was even more motivated to go.

Activity

Climb the stress-free ladder

You've identified one key area of your life that you find stressful. Take a look at the ladder below and focus on some small steps that you could take to reduce your stress levels in the area you've identified. See how far up the ladder you can get – moving away from stressful and towards stress-free – by inserting one practical thing you can do to help your climb.

Here's the ladder a mum of three completed. The area she identified was significant relationships – her relationship with her partner.

Now complete your own ladder.

STRESS-FREE

- Tell him what he does well as a dad.
- Talk about things other than children.
- Talk more feelings and less facts.
- Go to a football match with him.
- Give him a cuddle.
- Stop criticising him – especially about the small things.
- Remind myself what I love about him.
- Tell him what I love about him.
- Arrange a babysitter so we can go out.
- Tell him that I love him.

STRESSFUL

STRESS-FREE

STRESSFUL

DAY 49: FACT VERSUS FEAR

Many parents report that when they have a family, they find their anxiety levels rise significantly. They begin to worry about all sorts of things that they never used to give a second thought to. They may be small worries – or major ones. Lots of mums and dads, for example, say that having a baby has really made them focus on their own mortality.

It's easy to understand why. Being responsible for yourself is one thing. Being responsible for a child is quite another. The stakes are much higher. Being a parent is the most important job you'll do in your life.

Parents can find their stress levels rise because they live in a world of fear – not fact. If you're equipped with the facts about issues, you're in a position of strength. You are well informed. You know what the risks are and what support is available. You're not letting your imagination run away with you. You're demonstrating great strength as a parent. You're prepared to take action and deal effectively with any challenge that you face in your family life.

TOP TIP

- If you're worried about something, find out the facts, keep informed and keep things in perspective.
- Be a great role model.
- Help your child cope with their fears by explaining the facts and helping them to keep things in perspective.
- The more you develop skills as a 'fact' parent, the more successful you'll be in managing stress.

'The central struggle of parenthood is to let our hopes for our children outweigh our fears.' Ellen Goodman, Pulitzer Prize-winning columnist

Activity

Are you a 'fear' or 'fact' parent?

Take a look at the features of a 'fear' parent and a 'fact' parent. Which one best describes you?

Fear parent

- Worries and does nothing
- Feels paralysed with fear
- Existing instead of living
- Imagination runs wild
- Feels isolated
- Worrying only increases stress levels

Fact parent

- Prepared to take action
- Moves forward with a purpose
- Living
- Imagination under control
- Enjoys strong support networks
- Dealing effectively with challenges reduces stress levels

As a parent, it's important that you create a strong support network for yourself. It's tough being a parent and there are lots of challenges. Building a positive community around you will help you to tackle them much more effectively.

Ask for support

You may feel uncertain about asking for support. Don't. You may feel that you should be able to deal with everything yourself. Don't. Asking for support is a sign of family strength – not weakness. You do it because you care. You want to be the best parent you can be.

Different types of support

- Advice about a parenting problem
- Information or advice about health, childcare or education
- Practical support in the home
- Help with childcare logistics
- Emotional support – someone to talk to

Sources of support

- Health professionals
- Childcare professionals
- Education professionals
- Support groups
- Charities
- Websites
- Partner
- Family
- Friends
- Other parents

Activity

Focus on your support needs

Think about the challenges that you are facing as a parent at the moment. What specific support would help to reduce your stress levels?

1. Identify one specific area where support would help you.
2. Write down exactly what support you want.
3. Decide who is the best person/organisation to ask.
4. Make a note of any questions you want to ask.
5. Call them today.

It may mean a friend or grandparent looking after your child so that you get to the shops. Or asking your partner – if you have one – to play a more active role in sharing your sleepless nights. Make that call. Remember that together you are stronger.

Your notes

CHAPTER 11

DE-JUNK FAMILY LIFE

DAY 51: SURVEY THE CRIME SCENE

As a parent, you'll know all about accumulating clutter. There are so many bits and pieces that come with a new arrival – nappies, toys, prams, baby alarms, and bottles. Sometimes it can be a logistical challenge just finding a place to park the baby!

How one so small can create such great chaos and confusion is a question every parent asks. Their toys are everywhere – except the favourite one they're screaming for. You nearly break your neck on the pushchair as you squeeze past to get to the front door. Now you can't find the car keys because they're in a safe place… but where?

You don't need to have a perfect home – a messy home can be a fun home. This is about getting rid of what you don't want – and creating order.

Reasons to de-clutter

- Clutter drains your energy.
- Clutter increases your stress levels.
- Clutter can take control of your home.
- You'll feel more organised.
- You'll be more positive, energised and motivated.
- You'll enjoy clarity of thought.

Dealing with clutter is one of those things we never quite get around to – make today different!

Activity

Confront your clutter

1 Go into each room and write down one specific thing you want to de-clutter. Focus on the energy block in each room. It may be the children's toys, the furniture, the kitchen pin board, the bathroom cabinet or the endless pile of books.

2 Prioritise your clutter spots. Identify the number one clutter culprit on your list.

3 Go back to that room. Close your eyes and visualise what you would like it to look like in an ideal world. Focus on how good it feels.

TOP TIP

- Enjoy this experience. Be positive about it. The more clutter you have, the greater the difference you'll make!

DAY 52: THE NAPPY SACK CHALLENGE

You're going to really enjoy the next few days as you get to grips with tackling the junk that clutters your family home. It's a great thing to do and – by the end of today – you're guaranteed to feel great!

As a parent, you have a huge amount to think about every minute of every day. It can be hard to think straight. If your surroundings are cluttered and chaotic, it's even harder. It's time to change all that and bring order to your home and thoughts.

Activity

Start small

It's time to sort out your handbag or baby/child rucksack. Be careful, you never know what lurks in the dark corners that haven't seen the light of day for months!

Take a nappy sack (or small carrier bag) and fill it with rubbish from your handbag or your child's rucksack. Empty everything out onto a piece of newspaper and take a good look at what's there. Sort it out. Fill the sack with rubbish. Get rid of anything that you don't use or that's broken. Only put back the things that you feel really good about having there and that are there for a specific purpose.

TOP TIP

- If this activity really motivates you, seize the moment and clear out the car. Journeys can be stressful times for parents with demanding children, and a de-cluttered car will help you feel calm.

Real mum's advice

Get into the habit of de-cluttering your child's rucksack at the end of each day and packing it ready for your next family adventure. It only takes a few minutes and you'll feel good about being prepared.

DAY 53: CLUTTER CULPRIT... THEIR BEDROOM

Today you're going to tackle a major energy drain in your home – your child's bedroom. You know – the place where the toy boxes have developed a life of their own and half-eaten breadsticks lurk under the bed!

Your child may be tiny but they already seem to have more toys and clothes than a major department store. They've lots of outfits to wear – but usually end up in the same clothes. It's time to get sorted.

Try to be objective rather than emotional as you have a sort out. You can't keep everything. Make positive decisions about what you want to stay. Follow these simple steps... and enjoy!

TOP TIP

- Don't try to do this with your child's help. As you put one thing in the bin bag... they'll take it out! Ask your partner, friend or your child's grandparents to look after the children – and throw yourself into the challenge.

Activity

Imagine a clear, decluttered room

Visualise what the room will look like once it's been de-cluttered.

1 Remove anything that doesn't belong in the room. Think about different ways of arranging the room and experiment with space.

2 Throw away any broken toys. Put toys that your child has outgrown or never uses into a 'charity' pile. Create a 'fun area' with favourite toys and books. It's important for your child to know that the bedroom isn't just the place to sleep.

3 Label toy boxes and create a system. It will help your child develop organisational skills and understand how to group toys in different ways.

Real mum's advice

If there are toys, etc. in *your* bedroom, take them out. Keep your bedroom as free of child clutter as possible and it will help you to relax and sleep – even if your child spends a lot of time in bed with you.

DAY 54: DE-CLUTTER THEIR CLOTHES

It's amazing how many clothes your child will accumulate. They grow out of them so quickly that you're constantly adding to the collection. The wardrobe is full, the drawers are bursting at the seams. And there are still piles of clothes on the bedroom floor, in the TV room and on the stairs.

In a few days we are going to de-clutter your wardrobe (Day 69). But, for today, we are going to concentrate on the children's clothes. Not only will you feel more organised and in control, it will mean that you feel less stressed when you're trying to get your child dressed in a hurry.

TOP TIP

- Use children's hangers.
- Use plastic clothes storage bags that can go under the bed.
- Put a hook on the back of your door for extra storage if there's not one there already.
- Find a good home for the clothes you don't want – perhaps a charity or another mum.

Real mum's advice

Get into the habit of preparing your child's clothes the night before if you're always rushed in the morning.

Activity

Plan a clothes system

Take all of the children's clothes out of the wardrobe and drawers and decide on a clothes system that works for you. Just because you've always put pants and vests in one place doesn't mean it's the best place. Clear the storage space and then decide how you want to fill it.

In

- A clothes system that works for you, instead of clutter that doesn't
- Get out those clothes you keep for best – and get wear out of them
- Sort out outfits with matching tops/bottoms and keep them together
- All accessories in one place, for example, hair clips, belts, etc

Out

- All outgrown clothes
- All clothes not worn or that you don't like
- Any pants or vests you really don't need (don't keep seventy if seven will do!)
- All single socks you've been hanging onto in case the other one turns up

DAY 55: DE-CLUTTER YOUR MIND

You've done lots of great work to de-junk the family home and you'll already be noticing the positive effects.

You're creating clarity in the home and developing a frame of mind that's clear, positive and focused. Everyone benefits – you, the family and the charity shops.

Activity

De-junk your mind

It's time now to go to the next level and really enjoy de-cluttering your mind. You've probably been so busy since you started a family that you haven't had time to stop and think. Your head is probably full with so many thoughts – the housework, the to-do lists, the shopping, etc ...It's time now to de-clutter your mind and focus on what's really important in your life.

1 Close your eyes, breathe deeply and concentrate on feeling every breath.

2 Start to de-junk your busy mind – just as you have de-junked your home. Focus on your mind as an empty room that you can fill with whatever you want to.

3 Fill the space with positive thoughts about what's really important to you as a mum or a dad.

4 Enjoy the sense of calm as you concentrate on what you love most about your family.

Get into the habit of de-junking your mind at least once a day.

TOP TIP

- Now you're feeling energised, challenge yourself to tackle one of your clutter hotspots. Choose your target, grab a dustbin liner and set yourself a time limit of ten minutes to see what a difference you can make.

Real mum's advice

I got my husband to take the children to the park and blitzed the house. I managed to fill five black bin liners without trying. When he came back my husband commented on how well I looked and asked if I'd had a sleep! The house looked great and I felt great – and the children didn't notice that I'd cleared out their toy boxes.

Your notes

CHAPTER 12

TAKE CONTROL AND ORGANISE YOUR LIFE

'There just isn't enough time to do everything!' is the popular battle cry of many parents. The clock is like a time bomb ticking away, warning you that you're just never going to fit everything in, no matter how hard you work at it.

Stop letting the clock control you. Today is the day you take control of the clock and start to make positive decisions about how you choose to use your time.

Frantic parent = frantic child

If you're a frantic parent, your child will grow up believing there are never enough hours in the day.

Relaxed parent = relaxed child

Teach them a great lesson in life instead – that time is precious and it's important to value every minute of the day.

'Slow down and enjoy life. It's not only the scenery you miss by going too fast – you also miss the sense of where you are going and why.' Eddie Cantor, US comedian (1892–1964)

TOP TIP

- You're in control of your time, so decide what you want to do with it. If you believe you can take control and organise your life, you will. If you believe you can't, you won't. The decision is yours.

Activity

How do you spend your time?

If you're going to make changes, it's important to start by finding out how you spend your time now.

Choose a day you want to focus on – either a week day or weekend. Write down how many hours you spend on each of the following activities:

	Hours
• Going out to work	______
• Housework	______
• Chores outside the home, for example, shopping	______
• Sleeping	______
• Watching TV	______
• 'Me' time	______
• Family activities, for example, mealtimes, bedtime, bathtime	______
• Playing/reading with child – quality time	______
• Other – please specify	______
Total	**24 hours**

Now show this information in a different way. Each space below represents one hour of your day. If, for example, you spend eight hours sleeping – lucky you! – write sleep in eight of the boxes, etc.

What activity would you like to spend one hour more doing?
What activity could you spend one hour less doing?

DAY 57: MAKE YOUR 'TO DO' LIST MANAGEABLE

One of my clients, a mum called Katie, once likened her 'to do' list to the daleks in Dr Who. I knew just what she meant. Instead of helping her organise her time, her 'to do' list had become her arch enemy. It was always there, threatening to make her life more difficult. Her 'to do' list controlled her. She didn't control it.

There's nothing more stressful than a 'to do' list that's out of control. You just know you'll just never get to the bottom of it.

TOP TIP

- Instead of thinking about what you *need* to do, consider what you *want* to achieve. You're much more motivated by wants than needs. If you want to do something, you'll always find a way to make it happen.

Real mum's advice

I stopped writing a 'to do' list and started thinking about one important thing to achieve each day. I told my partner what I was going to do over breakfast – and reported back at bedtime. It was fun – and now he does it too.

Activity

Think 'achievement' not 'to do' list

In the following table, write down what you want to achieve today under the headings of 'Parent' and 'Chores'. Fill as many of the spaces as you want to.

A 'to do' list is usually dominated by chores we *need* to do. We don't often spend time thinking, for example, about what we *want* to achieve as a parent. Enjoy spending a few minutes doing this.

Instead of putting them all together in one list, break down the bigger picture and take a look at it.

Parent	Priority	Chores	Priority

Now organise your list by indicating your top priority in each area. Set yourself a goal. My challenge to you is to achieve your top parent and chore priorities by the end of today. Be a goal scorer – and give 'to do' lists the red card!

DAY 58: DO... DELEGATE... OR DUMP!

There are lots of reasons why parents have too much to do and too little time to do it. Here are the top two reasons:

1 Parents will try to do everything themselves because it's usually easier and quicker than delegating to another family team member.
2 Mums and dads are so frantic that they usually don't stop to think about their priorities and what they want to achieve. They try to knock as many things off the list as possible.

TOP TIP

- An effective family team leader will:
  - do what they want to do or what only *they* can do
  - delegate where necessary
  - prioritise activities instead of trying to do all of them
  - prioritise and focus on the important ones.

By being an effective family team leader, you're teaching members of your family life skills that they can use.

'Acting is just a way of making a living, the family is life.'
Denzel Washington, actor

Activity

Write down an achievement list

Write down your achievement list for today. Now go through each list and for each item decide if:

- you want to do it
- you can delegate it to someone else
- you're going to dump it.

Write down 'Do', 'Delegate' or 'Dump' for each activity.

Parent	Do Delegate Dump?	Chores	Do Delegate Dump?

How much time will you save by dumping or delegating chores? Now you can spend that time doing what you want to do as a parent.

DAY 59: TIME-CREATION IDEAS

You've already achieved a great deal in this chapter. You'll be feeling energised and liberated as you take control of the clock. You're doing more of the things you want to achieve as a parent. You know that you can make choices and that by taking control of your time, you're moving closer to being the parent you want to be.

Activity

Top 20 tips to create more time

Take a look at these top 20 tips to create more time to do the things you want to do. Use the ones that work for you.

1 Stock up on ready-made meals or order a takeaway.

2 Stop talking about 'lack of time'.

3 Start talking about what you achieve with your time.

4 Set the alarm ten minutes earlier and plan your day over a cup of tea.

5 Leave work on time. If you don't put your family first, no-one else will.

6 Leave your mobile at home when you take the children out.

7 Consider going part-time or changing your job.

8 Use the quick wash and don't iron.

9 Pack your baby rucksack the night before an outing.

10 Set up a support network with other mums and give each other time off.

11 Cut down on your child's social life.

12 Watch less TV.

13 Ask the grandparents to babysit on a regular basis.

14 Buy shopping and presents online.

15 Walk instead of driving – you keep fit and can concentrate on talking to the children.

16 Use a family diary to prioritise your time.

17 Stop saying, 'Hurry up' to the children.

18 Stop saying, 'We're going to be late'.

19 Go to bed thinking about what you're looking forward to tomorrow.

20 Enjoy being a parent. Slow down and treasure every moment.

TOP TIP

- Think simple not complicated. Read today's ideas thinking, 'Yes I could do that' instead of 'There are lots of reasons why I can't do that.'
- Stop seeing life in terms of 'saving time'. Start seeing life in terms of 'creating time'.

Real mum's advice

Learn to say 'no' when you want to. Don't put yourself and your family under pressure just because you feel you have to say 'yes'.

Spend your time with the people in your life who you really want to be with. Not only will you enjoy the experience more – you'll feel much more motivated to find the time to do it more often.

Spend time with upbeat people

As a mum or a dad, you're making decisions all the time. Choosing to spend time with the people you want to is a great decision. It takes planning. If you're not careful, you can end up spending hours with people who are negative and draining instead of with people who help you feel positive and motivated.

Don't spend time with mums just because they're mums with babies the same age. Choose the mums that share your vision and values. Avoid negative people and seek out the positive ones.

TOP TIP

- Make the arrangements today – not tomorrow. Choose one and put in a specific date and time and it will be much more likely to happen. When you're putting your date in the diary, tell the person you're arranging to meet what you appreciate about them – whether it's your child, your friend, your partner, your family or you. And while you're at it, book regular dates for the rest of the year. Plan and it will happen!

Activity

Plan your time carefully

Use your diary to plan the time you want to spend with the people that you want to be with. Be specific. Think about what you would like to do with them and for how long (for example, an hour, day, evening, weekend, etc). Visualise how much you'll enjoy it and you'll find the motivation to make it happen.

	Activity	Time required
Children		
Me		
Partner		
Family or in-laws		
Friend		
Other (specify)		

Your notes

CHAPTER 13

GET TO GRIPS WITH YOUR HOUSEWORK

DAY 61: SO MUCH TO DO... HOW STRESSED ARE YOU?

As a parent, you'll know just why a whole chapter in this book is devoted to housework. Many mums say that one of the key reasons they feel stressed and end up shouting at their children is because the grind of never-ending housework increases their stress levels. Instead of you controlling your housework, do you find that the housework is controlling you?

TOP TIP

- Get out and get some fresh air. The longer you spend in your home, the more stressed you'll feel about all that needs doing. Take your child and get out, even if it's just for a ten-minute walk. It'll blow away the cobwebs, you'll spend time with your child and the housework won't seem so important when you get back.

Real mum's advice

I decided to put my ironing pile in a cupboard and shut the door, so that it wasn't constantly staring me in the face. I felt much more relaxed immediately!

Activity

How does housework make you feel?

How stressed are you about the housework? In the table below are some of the most common words that mums say they feel when they think about the housework. Take a look at the list.

Focus on how you feel when you think about the housework. Take a look at each word and if it applies to you, score 1 stress point. If all of them apply to you, you'll have a 10/10 housework stress score.

	Score
• Out of control	________
• Tense	________
• Overwhelmed	________
• Guilty	________
• Failure	________
• Under pressure	________
• Disorganised	________
• Bad 'time manager'	________
• Tired	________
• Frantic	________
Total score	________

Your score

0–3: Low stress. You're in control of your housework.

4–7: You need to make changes.

8–10: Far too much stress. Your housework is controlling you.

DAY 62: CLEAN YOUR MIND – NOT YOUR LIVING ROOM

The reason you feel stressed about your housework lies in your mind – not your living room or kitchen. You want to be the perfect parent. You can spend hours… days… years trying to create the perfect family home. But you won't – because it doesn't exist. Family homes have families in them. Family homes are lived in. They have so many stories to tell. They're an integral part of your family adventure.

When your children are grown up with children of their own, you can rest assured that they won't be telling their families how well you made the beds. They'll be telling them about all the experiences you shared there as a family. They'll remember the fun family home – not the vacuumed home – forever.

TOP TIP

- Read your contract every day and remember what's really important in family life. Do you want the perfect house? Or a fun family home?

Activity

Sign up to a housework contract

Today's the day you commit to taking a different attitude to the housework. You may find it tougher than those toughest stains – but it's worth it. Take a look at this contract and if you agree with all the statements, sign it.

My Housework Contract

- I'll make good decisions about how I use my time.
- I want my children to grow up in a fun family home.
- I believe that a loving family home is more important than a perfect house.
- My relationship with my family is much more important than my relationship with the dishwasher.
- I'm in control of the housework.
- I'm motivated to limit the time I spend on the housework so I can spend more time with my family.

Signed: ______________________________

Date: __________________

DAY 63: TAKE CONTROL

The reason you feel your housework is spiralling out of control and your stress levels are rising is because you're letting it happen.

The importance of setting boundaries

One of the important lessons that we teach our children is to set boundaries. They're there for a reason. They provide a framework and security, and the freedom to enjoy life. So what stops you from doing that with your housework?

Commit today to take control. You can do it if you really want to.

Stop...

- believing the housework controls you
- thinking about the housework 24/7
- focusing on what you *haven't* managed to do.

Start...

- believing you're in control
- deciding to establish a routine with limits and a deadline
- focusing on what you *have* achieved.

TOP TIP

- If your time is up but you still have a strong urge to pick up the iron, remember that the housework will always be there – but your children won't always be at home. Once they've flown the nest, you'll have plenty of time to make your home look perfect.

Activity

Plan your housework

We often just 'do' the housework without thinking about it. We just get on with it. But if you take a few minutes to decide what you want to achieve in a set time, you'll always be more productive.

1 Set yourself a time limit for doing housework today. Be specific about exactly how long you're going to spend on it.

2 Make a list of what you want to achieve in that time and how long you want to allow for each task.

3 Do it – and stick to your deadlines. You'll be amazed by the results.

'At the worst, a house unkept cannot be so distressing as a life unlived.' Dame Rose Macaulay, author (1881–1958)

Real mum's advice

Make sure you have a great incentive to stop when your time is up – or you'll always find reasons to carry on. I always stop at 11am now and take my sons out for a walk – in rain or sunshine. We all love it. They're my incentive.

DAY 64: MANY HANDS MAKE FUN WORK

You probably think that housework is something that you 'have' to do while the children are asleep or busy elsewhere. The idea of involving them may strike fear into the heart of the strongest mum.

As parents, we're often on the look out for ways to spend time with our family and have fun with them. You want to get the housework done. So why not combine the two – go on, give it a go!

Sharing the housework with your little ones may take longer, but it will certainly have great advantages for both of you.

Advantages

- Precious talk-time
- More fun
- Puts housework in perspective
- Helps your child develop social skills
- Helps you and your child be creative
- Helps child sort, count, develop new language, etc.
- You can help your child see tidying up as a game not a pain
- Means children aren't watching TV
- Helps you enjoy being a parent

Activity

Share a task with your child

Choose one of your housework jobs today and share it with your child. What would you like it to be? Help with the cleaning, cooking or shopping? Commit to making it a positive experience that you share with them – and do it!

TOP TIP

- Enjoy the new perspective. Don't think about how much longer it's taking you – re-frame the activity as a fun and shared experience. Watch out, you may even find yourself enjoying the cleaning too!

Real mum's advice

My daughter loves Cinderella. Now she loves helping me with the housework – and then we have great fun dancing together at our own Cinderella ball when we've finished!

Hopefully you'll have enjoyed the activities over the past few days. Now you know that you can take control of your housework instead of letting it control you.

Rather than feeling stressed at the thought of everything that needs doing, you'll notice that you feel much more relaxed. There may still be 101 things around the home that need doing at some point – but you're in the driving seat and being the parent you want to be. You know now that if you're less tense about the housework, you're much less likely to feel stressed and negative with the children.

Activity

Check out how far you've come

Let's see just how far you've come in terms of taking control of the housework, decreasing your housework stress levels and boosting your energy. Are you still stressed by your housework? Or energised by the challenge?

Take a look at the table below. In the first column are the negative words that you focused on at the beginning of the chapter. In the second are positive words that may now replace the negative ones. Look at each line and circle either the negative word/phrase or the positive one. If, for example, you feel more relaxed instead of tense, circle 'relaxed', etc. Score one point for each word that you circle and add up your points at the end.

Negative = stress	Positive = energy
Out of control	In control
Tense	Relaxed
Overwhelmed	In perspective
Guilty	Good
Failure	Achiever
Stressed	Motivated
Disorganised	Organised
Bad 'time manager'	Good 'time manager'
Tired	Energised
Frantic	Fun
Stress score ____	**Energy score ____**

Your score
Higher stress score than energy score: You still have serious work to do. Get a life!
Higher energy score than stress score: Great. Your life has a balanced perspective.

TOP TIP

- Work smarter – not harder – every day.

Your notes

CHAPTER 14

BE A POSITIVE PARENT AND HAVE POSITIVE CHILDREN

Many parents say they find themselves living in a negative world. There's so much going on that their lives seem to be full of problems, not solutions. They find it easier to focus on reasons why things can't be done – than on reasons they can. It's not a world they want to inhabit. But they do. Welcome to family life…

It's not surprising. Being a mum or dad is tough. It can be hard work. It's a learning curve that changes on a daily basis – and sometimes the enormity of the challenge can really get to you.

Three good reasons to be a positive parent

- Optimists live longer than pessimists.
- You'll deal more effectively with family problems.
- You're more likely to have a positive child.

You can change your frame of mind and begin to respond more positively to the challenges of family life today. The decision is yours.

TOP TIP

- Get your day off to a great start. Find something good that happens before 9am every day.

Activity

Take a look at the table below. Each line has a negative and positive word or phrase in it. Circle the one that describes you most often. If, for example, you frown more often than you smile – circle 'Frowning', etc. Circle one word or phrase in every line. Score 1 point for every positive word or phrase circled.

Positive	Negative
Smiling	Frowning
Saying 'yes'	Saying 'no'
Fun	Frantic
Feeling good	Feeling guilty
Finding solutions	Seeing problems
Motivated	De-motivated
Standing tall	Stooped
Adventurous	Safe
Succeeding	Failing
'Can do'	'Can't do'
Score	**Score**

Your score
0–4: There's lots of work to do.
5–7: Enjoy raising your game.
8–10: You're a very positive parent. Good for you!

You decide how positive you are. It's not about what happens to you and what's outside your control. It's about *how you respond* to what happens to you. *You* determine your positive parenting rating.

Tell-tale signs of a negative parent

Do you:

- often use negative language about yourself as a parent?
- rarely use positive language about yourself as a parent?

Do you tell yourself and other people:

- what you haven't done?
- what you should have done?
- what you should do better?

Once you start to 'tune in' to what you say about yourself, you'll realise just how often you do the above.

If you're consistently using negative language about yourself as a parent, you're sending a powerful 'can't do' message to yourself and everyone around you. If you consistently use positive language about yourself as a parent, you're sending a powerful 'can do' message. The more you send it, the more you'll believe in yourself as a parent.

It's time to break the habits of a lifetime and be positive about what you achieve as a parent. Today's the day you talk yourself up instead of down.

Activity

Accept the elastic band challenge

Put an elastic band on your wrist. Every time you catch yourself saying something negative about yourself, ping the band to remind yourself that you're 'hurting' yourself with your words.

See how far through the day you can get without saying something negative about yourself.

TOP TIP

- Spend time with parents who are positive. Avoid the negative parents – negativity can be catching.

Real mum's advice

I only managed to get through to 6.30am on the first day but I really enjoyed getting through to 9am the next. I was shocked to realise that I kept saying, 'I'm a bad mother.'

DAY 68: TALK YOURSELF UP

So now you've stopped all that negative stuff about yourself, what on earth are you going to talk about?

Focus on the positives

Being positive about yourself and your role as a parent may feel odd – because you hardly ever do it. Give it a go today and enjoy the challenge.

- Instead of telling other people what you haven't done, tell them what you have achieved.
- Instead of telling them what's going wrong, tell them what's going well.
- Instead of telling them what you're feeling stressed about, tell them what you feel good about.
- Instead of telling them what makes you anxious, tell them what you love about being a parent.
- Instead of telling them you never have any time, tell them what you enjoy doing when you're with your children.

It's a frame of mind that you can get into if you want to. Talk positively about being a mum or dad today and you'll notice immediate results. It'll be good for you – and good for everyone you meet.

TOP TIP

- Take a second to think about what you're going to say before you say it and think about the words you'll use.
- Remember that by changing your habits, you're helping your child. If they hear you talking yourself down all the time, that's what they'll do. If they hear you being positive about yourself and what you achieve, they'll do the same about themselves.

Activity

Remind yourself how well you're doing

Have a pad of yellow stickies with you all day today. Whenever you manage to say something positive about yourself as a parent, write it down on one of the stickies.

In the evening, put those yellow stickies in a place where they're easily seen. It could be on the fridge or on the mirror in your bedroom. Leave them there for 24 hours. Every time you look at them – remind yourself what a great job you do.

'Nothing has a stronger influence psychologically on their environment and especially on their children than the unlived life of the parent.' Carl Jung, Swiss psychiatrist (1875–1961)

Real mum's advice

I've really changed my habits and I love asking other mums positive questions too. I love being the one who gets them to talk positively about what a great job they do. School pick-up time is really uplifting now.

DAY 69: HAVE A POSITIVE BODY

It's time to get up close and personal and take a good, positive look at your body. You may love being a mum. But when you look in the mirror, you might feel tired and frumpy. You see black bags under your eyes and a spare tyre around your tummy. Your clothes are loose instead of fitted – just in case you put on an extra pound or two.

Or perhaps you're a dad who's finding broken nights a form of torture and you don't have the energy to get out of the home for a drink with the lads – let alone a circuit at the gym. Your body's become less of a six pack… and more economy barrel!

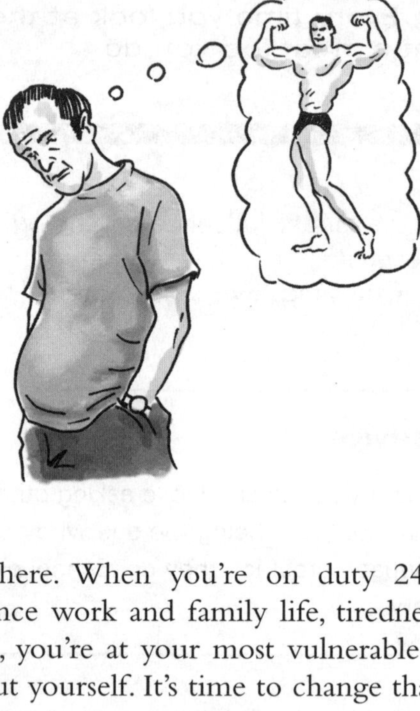

We've all been there. When you're on duty 24 hours a day or struggling to balance work and family life, tiredness kicks in. When you feel shattered, you're at your most vulnerable and you can feel very negative about yourself. It's time to change that.

Activity

Me or frazzled parent

It's time to clear out your wardrobe. Take out all of the clothes that you don't feel great in. As you try them on, take a look and decide, 'Is this me or is this frazzled parent?' Me stays. Frazzled parent goes. Only keep the clothes and colours that you feel positive in – give the rest to charity.

You'll have plenty of space now to treat yourself to that new outfit.

TOP TIP

- Whenever you look in the mirror, remember that changes in your body show you're on an amazing journey – parenthood. Cuddle your child and your partner – if you have one. They love you for being you.

Real mum's advice

I joined a great exercise class. It was in the park and we used our babies in their prams and pushchairs as part of the routine. I felt much healthier and made some good friends.

We live in a world where people are constantly talking about what they'd like to have and how their life would be better and different if they had it.

As a parent, it can be tempting to fall into that trap. I'd feel happy if… I had a bigger home for all our stuff… If I worked nearer home… If I gave up work… If I had a new washing machine. With that frame of mind, it's easy to end up feeling negative about life as it is now, just because you don't have everything on your wish list.

It's true that some of these things might make your life a little easier. But they won't transform an unhappy person into a happy one or a negative one into a positive one.

Live for today – not tomorrow

The key to being a positive parent is to appreciate everything you have here *today*. It's about recognising the value of your family *now*.

It may seem a long way off – but the time will quickly come when your children are grown up and have left home. Appreciate everything they bring to your life now and treasure every moment. The key is to be happy now – and your children will be too. Happiness is a journey, not a destination, so seize the moment and celebrate all that's good in your life instead of dwelling on what's missing.

Activity

Focus on the good things about being a parent

Take a look at the word 'parent'. Take one letter of the word at a time. Write down something beginning with that letter that makes you feel positive about being a parent today.

P	
A	
R	
E	
N	
T	

TOP TIP

- Treat every day with your child as though it was your last day with them and you'll treasure every moment you share with them.

'Very little is needed to make a happy life.' Marcus Aurelius Antoninus, Roman emperor and philosopher (121AD–180AD)

Your notes

CHAPTER 15

ENJOY BEING IMPERFECT

DAY 71: UNDER PRESSURE TO BE THE 'PERFECT PARENT'

There's enormous pressure on you to be the perfect parent. It's everywhere you turn. There are reports on the television about what your child should or shouldn't eat. There's a special on the radio about working mums failing their children. And your newspaper assures you that every hour your child spends watching videos will have harmful effects.

When your TV is on or you flick through a magazine, all you seem to see are adverts showing images of perfect parents with perfect children.

On top of that, you have people lining up to give you advice about what you should be doing with your children – your family, friends, mums at your parent–toddler group and sometimes complete strangers in the supermarket!

The 'perfect parent' is a myth. Neither the perfect parent nor the perfect child exists. So, stop trying to be the perfect parent because you're trying to achieve something that's impossible.

Activity

Tune into media pressure

Tune in today to the powerful messages that the media is sending you about being the 'perfect' mum or dad.

As you read a story, see a news report or listen to the radio, remember that a 'bad news' story about what parents have to feel anxious about is usually more attractive to the media than a 'good news' story about what they're all doing well. In the media, guilt is much sexier than good.

The first step to dealing with the pressure you're under is to acknowledge just how intense it can be.

DAY 71: UNDER PRESSURE TO BE THE 'PERFECT PARENT'

TOP TIP

- Today is the day you stop giving yourself a hard time trying to be perfect and give yourself permission to enjoy yourself – being imperfect!

Real mum's advice

When I hear a news story about working mums and guilt, I turn the radio off or listen to something different. I'm doing the best I can.

'No matter how calmly you try to referee, parenting will eventually produce bizarre behaviour, and I'm not talking about the kids. Their behaviour is always normal.' Bill Crosby, actor, producer and comedian

DAY 72: YOUR IDEA OF 'THE PERFECT PARENT'

On top of all of the external pressure to be the perfect parent – which is bad enough – there's you to contend with. It's easy to understand why you put yourself under huge pressure to be the 'perfect parent'. You only have one shot at this with your child and the stakes are incredibly high. Being responsible for yourself is one thing. But you're also responsible for a child who's dependent on you. The pressure is on.

TOP TIP

- Focus on the qualities that you admire in yourself and celebrate what you achieve as a parent.
- By focusing on the qualities you admire in other parents, you're already prioritising them as qualities you'd like to develop in yourself. You're identifying what's important and on the way to boosting this quality in you.

Real dad's advice

I decided that I wanted to be Mr. Incredible and take my children on more adventures. We'd got stuck in a rut. It's been fantastic for all of us – especially our camping trips.

Activity

What's your best quality as a parent?

Focus on your single greatest quality as a parent. Write it in the table below.

Now think of two people who you regard as great parents in some way. You might choose your own mum or dad. Or a parent that you know. Perhaps you'd pick a parent from a film or TV show that you're familiar with. Or a high-profile parent who's been in the news.

Focus on each one in turn and identify the one specific quality that you admire about them and write it down. What's the one thing that stands out about them as a parent?

Parent's name	Quality you admire in them
Me	

The next step is to put yourself in your child's shoes and see the world through their eyes. What do you think their idea of the 'perfect mum or dad' would be?

Dig the dirt

As a mum or dad, what's your first reaction to the word 'dirt'? You may think of piles of washing, germs or hard work cleaning carpets. But your child's much more likely to associate the word with fun!

- You may think, 'messy kitchen'. They may think, 'What a great painting session!'
- You may think, 'untidy bedroom'. They may think, 'What fun I've had creating a palace here!'
- You may think, 'toothpaste on the wall'. They may think, 'Great – Dad's letting me be independent!'

It doesn't matter how old your child is. See the world through their eyes and you'll see that your view and their view of a perfect parent may be quite different. For children, the time you spend with them and the attention you give them is the priority. It's about what you do that's fun and builds great memories. We can learn a lot from them.

TOP TIP

- Your child loves you unconditionally. In their eyes, you'll always be the perfect parent – imperfections and all. Enjoy.

Activity

Step into your child's shoes

Think about your child and what they look for in a parent. Complete the table below by filling in one thing that you do that makes you a 'perfect parent' in their eyes – you accumulate a point for each positive quality you demonstrate. Be specific. Instead of, for example, writing 'spend time with them', write down exactly what they would like to spend time doing with you. Make it easy for yourself to be perfect. Giving them a cuddle or a smile can add a point to your score sheet. Enjoy writing your list – and achieving a well-deserved 10/10!

Your perfect parent factor	Score out of 10
	1/10
	2/10
	3/10
	4/10
	5/10
	6/10
	7/10
	8/10
	9/10
	10/10 Excellent

So now you've made important leaps forward. You've stopped being the perfect parent and you're beginning to really enjoy being the parent that your child loves.

There's no such thing as a perfect parent – and there's no such thing as a perfect child either. Just imagine what life would be like if you were the mum or dad to the perfect son or daughter. How would you feel? Would you enjoy the adventure half as much as you do now?

Your child is a little person and you're in the fantastic position of being able to excite them about the world. You can channel their energy and enthusiasm. You help to create the adults they become.

Love their imperfections

If you put yourself under pressure to have the perfect child, you'll fail again. It can't be done. Spend your time, instead, appreciating all that you love about them – imperfections and all.

TOP TIP

- Enjoy supporting your child's special character and interests as they grow older. Let them be the child they want to be – not the child you want them to become.

Activity

Notice your child's uniqueness

Your child is an independent spirit. They have their own personality and their own character. They're growing and changing every day. Your child is special and unique. Tune into your child today and answer the following three questions.

1. What is it about them that constantly surprises you?
2. What do you see when you look into their eyes?
3. What is it about them that will make you forgive anything?

Real mum's advice

Stop comparing your child to other children and siblings. I kept saying to Harry, 'Why can't you be more like your sister?' until one day he turned to me and said, 'You love her more than me, don't you?' Of course that wasn't true but I knew where he was coming from.

DAY 75: BOOST YOUR IMPERFECTIONS!

An imperfect parent is a fun parent – so be on the lookout to boost your imperfections. It'll do you and your family the world of good.

Get into the right frame of mind. An imperfect home is an interesting home. A less than perfectly tidy bedroom is a world of adventure. A slightly messy fridge means dinner will always be a surprise.

TOP TIP

- Feel great, not guilty. You're prioritising your time and spending it being a great parent.

Real mum's advice

I always used to carry my mobile with me and leave it switched on. If it rang, I answered it even if it was my time with my daughter. My advice is: Get out of the home and leave your mobile at home!

Activity

Have a break!

Think about the way you spend your time at the moment and what you least like doing. Instead of spending an hour on that activity, you're going to have fun with your child. It'll be naughty – but nice. Here are some ideas to get you started.

- Forget the ironing.
- Leave the washing in the laundry basket.
- Get a ready-made meal for tonight.
- Let your baby wear a T-shirt with food stains.
- Switch your answering machine on.
- Ignore the dishes in the sink.
- Leave the beds unmade.
- Tidy the toys only once today.

This is what I'm definitely *not* going to do:

This is what I'm *definitely* going to do instead:

Your notes

CHAPTER 16

LIVE FOR TODAY AND LEAVE THE PAST BEHIND

One obstacle to enjoying family life to the full can be a parent's tendency to hang on to what's happened in the past rather than letting go and moving forward.

It may be earlier in the day, last week – or years ago. Parents are skilled at using up huge amounts of time and energy feeling bad about something that's been and gone. It may be something you said – or didn't say. It may be giving up breastfeeding or going back to work. It may be a row in front of the children. It may be a separation or divorce.

Are you a 'what if' or a 'what now' parent?

You can't change the past. By dwelling on what's gone, you become a 'what if' parent… 'What if I'd done this or not done that?' As a 'what if' parent, you're wasting energy. You're standing still. Only look back if that's the way you want to go.

But you can change the present and you can create the future. Be a 'what now' parent who enjoys the present and looks forward to the future. 'What now' parents know where they're going and move forward.

Activity

Your three-minute vision

Brainstorm all the things that you have to look forward to in the future as a mum or dad – and write them down. Be creative and think blue skies!

'Change your thoughts and you change your world.' Norman Vincent Peale (1898–1993), motivational author

TOP TIP

- Take a maximum of three minutes to complete today's activity – you'll be amazed at just how much joy the future holds for you!

DAY 77: MOVING FORWARD

Of course, our past is very important to us. The life experiences and the relationships we've had all shape the kind of person we are today.

Hold on to the bits of the past you want to bring with you into family life and into your future. And deal with the parts that are holding you back and stopping you from moving forward.

TOP TIP

- If you want professional help to help you deal with an issue that you struggle with, consult a specialist in the field.

Real mum's advice

Make sure you don't become your mother. Be on the lookout for developing habits that used to irritate you about your parents. I realised that I'd developed my mum's irritating habit of calling my children by the wrong name! Now I think about what I loved most about Mum – and I'm committed to developing only the habits I loved about her, not the ones that irritated me.

Activity

Ten steps to move forward

Stand in front of a mirror and say the following statements out loud to yourself.

1 I acknowledge there are things that have happened in the past that I have done or said as a parent that I struggle with.

2 I'm committed to moving forward.

3 I recognise that I can't change other people but I can change myself.

4 I'm a powerful role model and want my child to learn from me.

5 I will help myself and my family by letting go of negative feelings that I have for other people and myself.

6 I have a great deal to offer to my children.

7 I have a range of personal qualities that will help me create an exciting future.

8 I want to create a positive future for my family and the starting point is me.

9 I'm excited about enjoying the future.

10 I'm in control of my destiny.

DAY 78: FAILURE ISN'T AN OPTION

In a survey by the national charity Parentalk, two out of three parents believed they were *failing* in their role. This is because people set the bar so high that they're bound to fail – that 'perfect parent' syndrome again.

Feelings of failure or fear of failure are powerful. They can paralyse you and your children and stop you from moving forward. We grow up judging our lives in terms of success and failure.

If you want your child to grow up believing that life isn't black and white – that it isn't a case of success or failure but a rich and valuable learning experience – you'd better start believing it yourself. Failure isn't an option. Focus on what you can learn from every parenting experience and you'll develop skills and move forward.

TOP TIP

- Stop using the language of failure about your own life and your children will too. Challenge them when they say, 'I can't' and give them practical examples of their skills and qualities that will help them. Every experience is a learning experience. When it goes wrong, you've learned what not to do – or how to do it differently next time.

Activity

Focus on being a good role model

Focus on being a great role model today. It'll be good for you and great for your family. Every time you deal with something challenging, focus on how it's helping you develop your parental skills.

Do

- Talk positively about embracing the challenge
- Say 'I can'
- Feel positive
- Identify at least one positive thing you've learned from the experience
- Recognise that if you try something and it doesn't work, you're effectively reducing your options
- Find reasons for it to work
- Take responsibility for yourself

Don't

- Use the word 'fail'
- Say 'I can't'
- Feel anxious
- Dwell on all the things that went wrong
- See things that don't go according to plan as failures
- Find reasons for it not to have worked
- Look for ways to blame others

DAY 79: LIVE FOR THE MOMENT

The best way to appreciate all that you have as a mum or a dad is to live for the moment – not in the past – and live every minute to the full.

This is a challenge in today's busy world with so much going on and so many things to think about. There are so many distractions and 'to do' lists to add to that it can be hard to focus on what's happening in the here and now.

TOP TIP

- Find something to feel good about – about being a parent – before breakfast.
- Spend five minutes focusing on what you're looking forward to.
- Look at your children and recognise how lucky you are.

Activity

Connect to the child in you

When was the last time you got in touch with the child in you and saw the amazing world through a child's eyes?

Take a look at the activities listed in the table opposite and tick 'never', 'sometimes' or 'often' to indicate which applies to you.

Let's find out if you're up to speed when it comes to living in the moment.

	Never	Sometimes	Often
Left work on time to see the family			
Had a meal with your children without getting up			
Got down on the carpet and had a game at their level			
Enjoyed a real laugh with your children			
Felt so engaged with your children you forgot the stresses of life			
Got out of breath playing a physical activity with your family			
Did something you wanted to do with your children instead of something you needed to do in the home			
Cuddled your child because it's what you wanted to do more than anything in the world			
Followed your heart instead of your head			

Your score

Mostly never: Come on – life's too short!

Mostly sometimes: You know what fun it can be – do more.

Mostly often: Good for you – your children are lucky!

DAY 80: CREATE YOUR FAMILY'S FUTURE

The very best way to provide a happy future for your family is to create it for them. Don't leave it to chance. Family life is far too important for that. Most of us set ourselves targets in terms of the kind of job we'd like or income we'd like to be earning. We have goals about the holiday destinations we want to go on or the car we want to drive.

But when was the last time you set a goal for what you want to achieve as a parent? If you get into a car and start driving, it's unlikely you'll arrive where you want to go unless you've decided where that is in the first place.

The adults your children become are determined not by the school they go to or the exams they pass. The people they become will be shaped by the experiences you share with them – the holidays, the cuddles, the laughs, the books you've read together and the games you've shared.

TOP TIP

- Enjoy today's activity – it's what being a parent is really about!
- Be specific about the experience and give it a deadline, for example, '2pm on Saturday' instead of 'over the weekend'. Then it's more likely to happen.
- Don't talk about it – do it! It's the most important date in your diary.

'The art of parenting is to teach the art of living to children.'
Elain Heffner, writer

Activity

What do you want to do with your child?

Think about what you want to do with your child. What experiences do you want to share with them? A dream is a wish your heart makes.

Identify one experience you want to share with them in the next 24 hours.

____

____

Identify one experience you want to share with them in the next seven days.

____

____

Your notes

CHAPTER 17

PLAN IT – DON'T PANIC

DAY 81: DO YOU PLAN... OR PANIC?

Once you become a parent, you automatically go into planning mode. Your family becomes a complex logistical operation. You plan to survive. You plan in your sleep.

Expected planning

This covers routine planning to get you and your child through each day. Parents usually take day-to-day planning in their stride – practice makes perfect.

Planning for the unexpected

This is planning for those times when things don't quite go according to plan, for example your child being sick and you having to work. Most parents aren't strong on planning for the unexpected. They prefer to operate on the 'It won't happen to me' basis.

'In preparing for battle I have always found that plans are useless, but planning is indispensable.' Dwight D. Eisenhower (1890–1969), US General and Republican politician

TOP TIP

- The points in today's activity are key issues for you to address if you want to reduce stress levels. Each of them will take only between ten minutes and an hour to get to grips with.

Activity

How much of a planner are you?

Score one point for each statement you can say 'yes' to:

- I have set up emergency childcare.
- I keep a photo of my child in my wallet or handbag.
- I've got the contact numbers of two people to call in an emergency.
- I've got the contact numbers of my child's childminder or nursery.
- I know my family's monthly income and outgoings.
- I know the options available for my child at the next stage of their education.
- I've given all my contact details to anyone looking after my child.
- I've got the phone number of NHS Direct.
- I've made an up-to-date will that I'm happy with.
- I've left a set of spare house keys with two friends.

Total score ____________

Your score

0–3: You're a fire-fighter. There's high panic potential!

4–7: You're proactive in key areas.

8–10: You're in the driving seat. You plan and don't panic.

An 'it'll never happen to me' world can seem comfortable. Life seems easier like that – until the unexpected happens, of course. That's when you go into full panic mode. Your family life is suddenly out of control. You're no longer in the driving seat and stress levels can hit an all-time high.

If you know that you've planned and you're sorted, you can relax. Even if the unexpected happens, you can deal with it calmly.

Baby and child first-aid classes for parents and carers

Get peace of mind with a first-aid course. They're practical and you'll feel prepared to cope in a crisis. You could save your child's life. There are many organisations offering first-aid classes. Find out about one today – and book it.

- Ask your health visitor for details of local classes.
- Contact St John's Ambulance Lifesaver Babies and Children on 08700 10 49 50.
- Call your local branch of the Red Cross.

TOP TIP

- Speak to your employer about booking a health professional to run a first-aid class for parents at lunchtime. Many companies are keen to support parents in the workplace and this is a great way to help mums and dads.

Activity

Create an emergency notice board

Create an emergency notice board in your kitchen or somewhere very visible in your house. Put on it:

- the telephone number of NHS Direct (0845 4647)
- the contact number for your doctor
- the contact details of two people who can help in an emergency.

Store these details in your mobile or keep a copy in your handbag and, if you have a partner, give one to them to keep.

DAY 83: COPING WITH CHILDCARE EMERGENCIES

Coping with childcare emergencies are part and parcel of every parent's life. You can't predict every eventuality, but you can certainly be more prepared and therefore less inclined to panic.

It's going to happen to all of us one day.

Activity

Be prepared

Look at the following questions and see how many you can answer 'yes' to.

1. Do you know whether you – or your partner if you have one – would come home from work if the nursery called to say your child was ill and you needed to pick them up?

2. Do you know who would look after your child if you woke up and they were ill and you had to work?

3. Do you know who would look after your other child or children or do the nursery/school run if you were at home looking after a sick child?

If the answer to any of these questions is 'no', take action to turn that into a 'yes'.

Make sure that the contact details for everyone on your list are up to date.

TOP TIP

- Talk to all the people on your list and make sure they're happy for you to have them as emergency childcare contacts. Thank them for taking on that responsibility. We often take this for granted, but it'll help them feel valued and prepared for the moment they get that call.

Real mum's advice

Give your friends or family a house or flat key too. It may be easier for them to take your baby or child to your home instead of theirs while they're waiting for you to return.

Many parents say that once they have a family, they experience increased feelings of anxiety. Many report beginning to worry about their own mortality – and what would happen to their child if something happened to them.

Those feelings are absolutely natural. We all hope that we'll be around for as long as we can and see our children grow up and have happy lives with families of their own.

But it's vital that you have a will and that you're completely happy it. This may be tough, but you need to answer all the difficult questions. Your child deserves that.

Guardian angels

Think carefully about guardians. Who would you really want to bring up your children if you weren't around? Choose the people who share the same values as you and who you feel confident can provide the love you want for your child. It may be somebody in your family or it may be a good friend.

Whoever you choose, arrange a time to see them and ask them. Make sure you ask them to think about it and discuss it with anyone they need to – so that they have the opportunity to say no.

Activity

Check out your will

1. Find your will. If you haven't got one, arrange to write one this week.
2. Read it thoroughly – especially the section on guardians.
3. Discuss its contents with whoever you need to.
4. If your will needs changing, arrange it this week.

TOP TIP

- Always tell the person you're asking the specific reasons why you would like them to be guardians to your child – your most precious possession. Talk to them about the values, skills and qualities they have that have led you to make this important request.

DAY 85: FINANCIAL PEACE OF MIND

For many parents, it's the family finances – or lack of them – that can cause high levels of stress. Making ends meet can be a struggle, especially if you have to find extra cash to buy a pair of shoes or find the money for a school trip. You're stressed because your finances are controlling you instead of you controlling them.

Having a family is expensive. But the experience of being a mum or a dad is priceless.

If you can get back into the financial driving seat, you'll feel in control and able to cope with financial challenges. Plan – don't panic about money.

TOP TIP

- Set yourself a budget for your shopping and stick to it. It will help you prioritise and be creative.

Activity

Sort out your finances

Step 1

Find out where all your money goes by filling in the table opposite. The major banks will usually give you a list of your current standing orders and direct debits to make this easier.

Step 2

Complete the following:

Total monthly income =
Total monthly outgoings =
Balance =

Step 3

Accept the budget challenge. If you had to reduce your monthly outgoings by £25 this month, how would you do it?

Step 4

Do it.

Monthly spending	£
Mortgage/rent	
House insurance policies	
Gas	
Electricity	
Water	
Council tax	
Life policies	
Telephone	
Television licence	
Satellite	
Car insurance	
Car bills	
Petrol/parking	
Travel	
Food	
Newspapers/magazines	
Entertainment	
Mobile	
Bank charges/debt	
Credit card bills	
Childcare	
Child-related expenses, e.g. clothes, nappies	
Savings	
Other (specify)	
Total monthly outgoings	

Real mum's advice
Buy all the supermarket's own brands one week. You'll save a fortune.

Real dad's advice
Cut up your credit cards.

Your notes

CHAPTER 18

LOOK AFTER THE 'REAL' YOU

DAY 86: YOU'RE THE HEART OF THE FAMILY – LOOK AFTER I

Being a parent is an extremely responsible job. You've got a lifelong commitment. Your natural instinct is to put your child first all of the time. After all, that's what parents are supposed to do, isn't it?

Mums in particular have a tendency to look after everyone else and put other people before themselves. It's not just their child, but their partner if they have one, their family, their friends, the neighbours – and even other families they know who are in need of a little support.

As a mum, you're great at looking after everyone else and not so good at looking after yourself. But it's vital that you nurture yourself. You are the heart of the family. If you're strong, the family will benefit. If you're weak, it will affect all of you.

Five good reasons for making 'me time'

- You'll live longer.
- You'll feel happier.
- You'll enjoy being a parent more.
- Your children will benefit.
- You deserve it!

TOP TIP

- Feel good about putting yourself first some of the time – it's the sign of being a great parent, not a guilty one.

Activity

How much time do you invest in you?

Take a look at the list of people that you look after, support and nurture. Rank them from 1–5 with number 1 being the person you invest most time and energy in and 5 the one you invest least time and energy in.

	Rank 1–5
Me	
Partner	
Family	
Friends	
Child or children	

Where do you come in the pecking order?

DAY 87: GIVE YOURSELF A MUM MAKEOVER

Today is the day to give yourself a real boost. It's time for you to nurture yourself. You're special and you deserve it.

How well do you look after yourself? Think about what you've done over the past seven days and answer the following questions. Award yourself 1 point for every 'yes'.

	Yes/No
• I had at least ten minutes of 'me time' every day	________
• I put myself before my child or partner.	________
• I enjoyed an evening out.	________
• I had a luxurious bath or pampered myself.	________
• I ate five portions of fruit/vegetables every day.	________
• I read a book, magazine or paper.	________
• I rang a good friend.	________
• I wore something I felt great in.	________
• I had an early night.	________
• I enjoyed doing some exercise.	________
Total score	________

Your score

0–3: You're not looking after yourself.
4–7: You're doing well – now raise your game
8–10: Excellent. You value yourself – and your family will benefit.

DAY 87: GIVE YOURSELF A MUM MAKEOVER

Activity

Plan a treat!

Choose one of the treats that you'd really like to have this week. Book it with your partner, family or friend – even if it's only for ten minutes – or it won't happen. Be specific about the day and time. Enjoy!

TOP TIP

As a busy mum, with little time, you get used to a make-up routine that takes minutes instead of hours. Sarah Jagger, *The Baby Channel's* Chief Make-Up Artist and presenter of *Mummy Makeover*, suggests these top tips:

- Forget mascara and dye your eyelashes!
- Banish dark circles with a concealer designed for the delicate eye area.
- Cheat a healthy glow by mixing equal portions of self-tan together with your moisturiser.
- For an instant skin 'pick-me up', steam your face over a bowl with two camomile teabags infused in boiling water.
- Throw out make-up products that are over a year old.
- Brush your lips gently with a dry toothbrush. It will get rid of dry patches and boost the blood flow, leaving you with a softer, plumper pout.

You will be a much better parent, more energised and more motivated if you nurture all aspects of you – not just the parent bit. Yes, being a parent may be the most important job you'll do in your life and having a family may affect everything you do – but it's not the whole story. Being a parent is part of the bigger picture of what you're all about.

Get in touch with 'you'

You don't have to be a parent 100 per cent of the time. In fact, if you take time out to be you and get in touch with all the other aspects of yourself, you're likely to be a better parent.

It's OK to take time out if you want to. It's good. It's positive. That's why 'me' time isn't a luxury – it's vital.

When you become a parent, you grow in lots of amazing ways as your special relationship with your child develops. Sometimes, though, some of the aspects you really enjoyed about yourself before you had children can disappear into the background.

Real mum's advice

We're always worrying about money. On the spur of the moment, I booked a house swap with a family in France. My husband couldn't believe it. It was one of the best holiday's we've ever had and it was really cheap. We only had to pay for the ferry.

Activity

Boost the qualities you've lost

In a Parent Coaching Academy survey, mums were asked to identify the top ten positive characteristics that they felt were no longer as strong, now that they had family responsibilities.

Take a look at the list and see if any of them apply to you.

- Unpredictable
- Adventurous
- Energetic
- Fun
- Optimistic
- Relaxed
- Easy going
- Flexible
- Calm
- Dynamic

TOP TIP

- The first step to boosting these lost qualities is to recognise that you want to. Choose one. Identify one specific thing that you can do to boost that quality in you today.

DAY 89: PICTURE YOUR DREAM

You're growing and developing in so many ways. Every day is a new and exciting experience. We're often so busy as mums or dads that we live from day to day and only plan ahead if it's necessary – the family holiday, the car MOT, the trip to the dentist.

Who do you want to be in the future?

The next step on your journey is to get in touch with who you want to be in the future and identify some of the experiences that will help you to achieve that.

As a parent, you may focus on your dreams for your child – but never forget your dreams for you. The first step to creating your dream is to dream it. If you don't have a goal to aim for in any area of your life, you're unlikely to hit it.

TOP TIP

- Spend five minutes every evening looking at the montage from today's activity and visualising the dreams you have for yourself. By focusing on what you want, you're bringing those dreams one step closer to becoming reality.
- Continue to add to your montage whenever you see an image that you'd like to add to your life to enrich it.
- Encourage your children to create their own life montage.

Activity

Make an aspirational montage

You'll need a plain piece of A4 paper and a pile of magazines and papers. As you look through them, think about what you want for yourself in the future. Whenever you see an image of how you want to be, cut it out and stick it on to your piece of paper. Gradually build up a montage full of images of what you aspire to be.

If, for example, you want to be very fit, you might use a picture of the Olympic athlete Kelly Holmes. If you want to be living by the sea, find a picture to represent it. If you want to boost your culinary skills perhaps a picture of Jamie Oliver. If you want a life full of happiness, use an image of the sun or great smiling faces.

This is for you. It contains all the elements that you want the future to hold for you.

DAY 90: TURN YOUR DREAM INTO A REALITY

It's time now to begin to turn your dreams into reality. You've completed your first step. In order to have a dream, it needs to be created.

In order to make your dreams come true, you need to focus on that dream and see it in your mind's eye in vivid colour. Paint the picture in your mind and enjoy the positive feelings it brings out in you.

Live your dream!

It can be a small goal or a huge one. The principle is the same.

D Set yourself a **D**eadline to achieve your goal.

R Make your goal **R**eal by imagining how great you will feel when you achieve it.

E Achieving the goal must **E**xcite you in some way as this will keep you motivated.

A Your goal must be **A**chievable. It can be as challenging as you like.

M Decide how you will **M**easure your goal. How will you know you've achieved it?

S Be **S**pecific. The more specific you are, the more likely it is to happen.

TOP TIP

- The more specific you are about the goal you want to achieve, the more likely you are to be successful.
- When you're helping your child to set goals, encourage them to be as specific as possible so that they can measure their success and recognise what they've achieved.

Activity

Focus on your goal

Focus on the goal or dream you want to achieve. Identify one that you'd like to achieve in the next week. Write it down.

My goal is:

____

____

Real mum's advice

I have started telling my best friend what my goal for the week is and she tells me hers. It's great to be able to tell her I've done it. Talking about it brings it one step closer and helps me be clear about what I want to do.

Your notes

CHAPTER 19

WIN THE WAR OF THE WORLDS

Your values are caught, not taught

Your values are the most powerful gifts you'll pass on to your children. Your values are 'caught', not 'taught'. If you want your child to develop good values and live those values on a daily basis, the starting point is you.

Living your values is key to your motivation. If you're acting in a way that conflicts with a value that's important to you, you're likely to feel de-motivated and unhappy. If you're really living your values, you're much more likely to be motivated and happy.

TOP TIP

- How does your child know what values are important in your life? What specifically do you do that demonstrates them? Every day we make decisions about how to live our lives. Today, focus on living your values – the ones you really want your child to catch from you.

Real mum's advice

I was having real problems with my teenager. I felt really cross because he wasn't treating me with any respect. But when I thought about it, I realised I wasn't showing him any either. I know I'm the adult and it's tough but I'm going to find ways to do it.

Activity

What do you value in life?

Focus on what you think is valuable in life. Below is a list of things that parents say they value in their lives and that are priorities in terms of what they want to pass on to their children.

- Love
- Health
- Honesty
- Adventure
- Respect
- Compassion
- Security
- Courage
- Happiness

Now answer these three questions:

1. Which of these is the most important to you?
2. Which is the one you'd most like to boost in your life?
3. What would you like to add to the list?

You've taken the time to think about the values that are important to you and that you want to pass on to your child. But how can you stop your loved one being affected by negative influences and people with values that are different from yours?

This isn't just a problem for the parents of teenagers – it's an issue for all parents.

The power of the media

In today's multi-media world, your child will come into contact with all sorts of people and be bombarded with messages on TV, through the internet, advertising and magazines. And, of course, you're not always with them. What happens if they get in with the 'wrong crowd', who might send powerful messages to your child?

Will your values be strong enough to see them through?

You can't always be with your child but you want them to have the confidence to say 'no' when they're faced with a situation that conflicts with the values that you've passed on to them. You want them to know the difference between right and wrong. You want them to know how to treat people.

TOP TIP

- There may be other influences on your child but you will be the most powerful role model. You may have stiff competition, but have the confidence to know that you're the most important influence in their life. The first step in seeing off the competition is to acknowledge it's there and decide to do something about it.

Activity

Consider the influences on your child

How worried are you about your child 'catching' the wrong values? Take a look at the list of influences that may affect your child. Consider each one in turn. If you're concerned about it having a negative impact on your child, score 1 point. If you're worried about all of them, your score will be 10 out of 10.

- TV
- Peers
- Advertising
- Internet
- Computer games
- DVDs
- Magazines
- Toys
- Other adults in their lives
- Books

Your score
0–3: Good – you're feeling confident.
4–7: You feel in control in certain areas.
8–10: You're worried. You feel you're losing control.

DAY 93: SETTING BOUNDARIES

As a parent, it's important to establish boundaries in family life. You'll have some boundaries that are negotiable and some that are non-negotiable.

Important reasons for setting boundaries

- Boundaries help your child know where they stand.
- Boundaries show that you care about them and what they're doing.
- Boundaries help them to feel secure and valued.
- Boundaries create a framework within which your child can grow and feel independent.

Toddlers and teenagers are just like us. They appreciate knowing that there is order. Their bedroom may look chaotic – but they don't want chaos in their own life. Of course, they'll try to push the boundaries – that's part of growing up. But they'd be lost if they weren't there.

The toddler times are a dress rehearsal for the teenage years. Be clear and consistent when they're young – and you'll have fewer challenges later on.

Activity

Check out your boundaries

Take a look at the list below. As you look at each of the influences on your child, ask yourself: 'Do I have clear and consistent boundaries in place that I have communicated positively to my child? Or are there inconsistencies that may send mixed messages to my child?'

- TV
- Screen games
- Toys

TOP TIP

- Know what your child is playing or watching.
- Decide which boundaries are negotiable and non-negotiable.
- Be positive in presenting boundaries.
- Be a great negotiator – say 'yes' more often than 'no'.
- Be a great role model – show them the value of give and take.
- Involve your child in setting the boundaries.
- Remember that you were a child once – put yourself in their shoes.
- Praise them for keeping to the boundaries.
- It's about telling them you care – not telling them what to do.

Real dad's advice

I was sending mixed messages to my son about watching TV because sometimes it was just easier to let him have his own way. Now I say to myself ABC: Always Be Consistent.

Lead by example

As a parent you may feel that you want your child to develop their own relationships and have the friends that they want – not the friends that you choose for them. But the foundations you lay for them are vital when it comes to helping them develop positive friendships and make great decisions about who they spend their time with.

You are their greatest 'friendship' role model.

Do you make a conscious effort to spend time with positive people who share your values and family vision? Or do you spend it hanging out with people who don't really share your values – but who have children of the same age so it's convenient and you can occasionally help with nursery pick ups?

If you want your child to develop positive and healthy relationships, it's important that you lead by example.

Real mum's advice

My daughter was refusing to share. I created a friendship sticker system and gave her one every time she did something positive with other toddlers. She loved it – she's like a different child.

Activity

Consider friendships

Take a look at the following questions. If you're strong in that area, score 3. If you're average, score 2. If there's lots of work to be done, score 1.

Do you...	Score
• Mix with people who share your values?	________
• Talk to your child about what you value about your friends?	________
• Talk to your child about what makes them a good friend?	________
• Talk to your child about what qualities they value in their friends?	________
• Create opportunities for your child to make new friends?	________
• Deal positively with your child's friendship struggles?	________
• Encourage your child to spend time in pursuit of a passion with like-minded people, for example football or drama?	________
• Avoid being negative about people?	________
Total score	________

Your score

1–7: Take immediate action!
8–15: Your child needs more guidance.
16–24: You're building a strong foundation.

DAY 95: GIVING AND RECEIVING

As a parent, you may want your child to be a good citizen, a good friend and an important part of the community. You may want them to learn the value of giving to others. It may be important that they learn that money can't buy you happiness; that time is more important than money.

Dos and don'ts

Do

- Spend time with them not money on them.
- Set boundaries in terms of the money you spend on them.
- Encourage them to give time to other people.

Don't

- Don't say 'yes' every time they ask for something in a shop – you're not doing yourself or them a favour.
- Don't say 'yes' to buying presents you can't afford.
- Don't give in to pressure – just because other parents are doing it.

TOP TIP

- Do it with an open heart – or not at all.

Activity

Give something back

Choose one thing that you and your child can do together to 'give something back' to the community.

- Make a card and send it to someone who could do with a cuddle.
- Clear out their bedroom – and yours – for charity.
- Run a shoebox sale with your child's toys to raise money for charity.
- Go to visit someone who would really appreciate it.
- Do a sponsored event together.
- Go and visit a charity that welcomes members of the public and talk to your child about the work that it does.

Real mum's advice

It was really tough the first time we sorted out toys James had outgrown to give to the charity shop, and I found it very challenging as a parent. But it made me really focus on what I wanted to say to James and how to say it. The second time was much easier.

Your notes

CHAPTER 20

LIFE, HERE I COME

You'll know by now that the most important message you'll take away from this book is that you are your child's most powerful role model. It's a responsibility that, at times, may seem overwhelming. but it means that every day you can have a positive impact on your child.

You are a powerful influence

You know that everything you say or do:

- affects the way they behave
- affects their relationships
- influences their development
- affects the person they grow up to be
- colours their view of the world.

TOP TIP

- Think about how far you have come since you started reading this book. You have made lots of positive changes that will make you an even better role model than you were at the beginning. Celebrate your achievements.

Activity

What makes you a great role model?

Draw a heart in the centre of a piece of paper and write 'I am' in the centre of it. Focus on the specific positive skills and qualities that make you a great role model for your child. Draw a line out from the heart and write one skill or quality that will finish the sentence, 'I am... '.

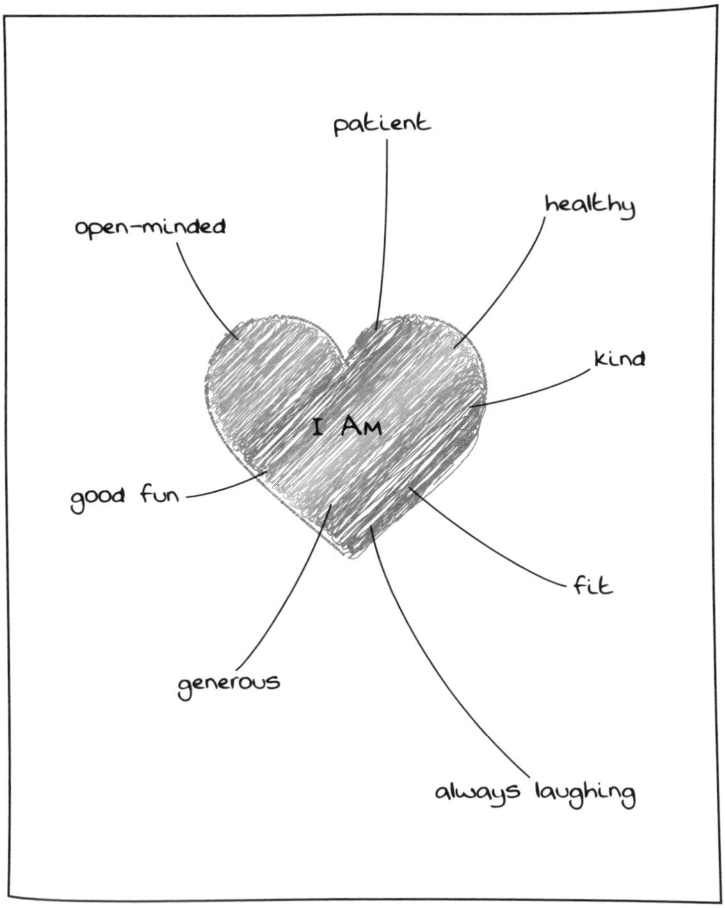

DAY 97: THE ONLY 'TO DO' LIST THAT MATTERS

As a parent, you know just how easy it is to keep adding to your 'to do' list, and we've worked on developing skills to make sure that you control your list rather than it controlling you.

It's time now to focus on the one 'to do' list that you have as a parent that really is important.

Take a few minutes to think about this activity and really enjoy brainstorming all of the possibilities.

TOP TIP

- Every experience that you share with your child will shape the person they become and the parent you are. Make these shared experiences your priority. The adult your child becomes isn't defined by their academic success. They're shaped by all the cuddles, laughs and challenges that you've shared together.

Real mum's advice

Tell your child what you want to do with them and ask them for their ideas too. Once you've told them, they will make sure you keep your word.

Activity

The important 'to do's

Write down one thing you want to do with your child before they start school.

Write down one thing you want to do with your child before they go to secondary school.

Write down one thing you want to do with your child before they leave home.

What can you do *today* to make your 'to do' list happen?

Every day you're teaching your child skills that they'll use for the rest of their lives. As you continue on this journey, you're enjoying the responsibility and challenge of being their most powerful role model.

Your child learns a lot about being a parent from you. They learn something every minute of every day that they're with you. That's an amazing place to be!

Activity

Pass on your wisdom

Close your eyes and visualise yourself in the future. You're enjoying being a grandparent now and your child has a family of their own. Picture the scene and paint it in your mind in vibrant colours. Imagine their children playing and laughing, and focus on how happy you feel.

If you could pass on one piece of advice to your child about being a mum or a dad, what would that one nugget be?

Write it down – and then take your own advice!

DAY 98: WHAT ADVICE DO YOU WANT TO GIVE YOUR CHILD?

Real mum's advice

I wanted to tell my child to have as much fun as they can every day. I realised that I just wasn't doing it myself. Now, every morning, I tell myself that I'm going to have fun today – and I tell my children so they can make sure I'm as good as my word.

Real dad's advice

Write down your words of wisdom and put them in every room of your house. They are so important they should be everywhere. I painted them on the wall in the garden.

DAY 99: CELEBRATE YOUR ACHIEVEMENTS

Well done! You're nearly at the end of your journey and, every day, you're moving one step closer to being the parent you want to be.

By now you'll know just how important it is to celebrate your achievements – and help your child to do the same. So let's take a few minutes to reflect on your success so far.

Activity

Check out how far you've come

Below are 20 key areas that you've focused on throughout this process. Take a look at all of them and score 1 point for each statement that you can say 'yes' to.

	Score
• I'm more sweet dreamer than screamer.	________
• I'm being the parent I want to be.	________
• I'm loving myself and my family.	________
• I'm developing tantrum-busting tips.	________
• I have volume control.	________
• I'm developing routines.	________
• I'm feeling good.	________
• I'm building my family team.	________
• I'm motivating and feeling motivated.	________
• I'm developing successful stress management strategies.	________

DAY 99: CELEBRATE YOUR ACHIEVEMENTS

	Score
• I'm de-junking family life.	________
• I'm taking control and organising my life.	________
• I'm getting to grips with the housework.	________
• I'm a positive parent.	________
• I enjoy being imperfect.	________
• I'm living for today.	________
• I'm planning – not panicking.	________
• I'm looking after the real me.	________
• I'm living my values.	________
• I'm looking forward to living the life I create.	________
Total score	________

How many areas were you able to say 'yes' to. How does that feel?

Congratulations. You're now at the end of your 100-day programme and well on the way to becoming the parent you want to be. You've come such a long way and achieved so much – taking one step, one day at a time.

Enjoy!

You're feeling relaxed, calm, happy, excited and confident about yourself and what the future will hold for you and your family. You know that there will be challenges along the way – and that overcoming them is part of the adventure of being a parent.

You're doing the most important job you'll ever do in your life. You've got a life – a really great life – and you're creating a special life for your child every day in everything that you do. Enjoy!

TOP TIP

- If you want to live your dream, create it and believe it!

'Happiness is when what you think, what you say, and what you do are in harmony.' Mahatma Gandhi (1869–1948)

Activity

Focus on your dreams, support and inspiration

Draw a large heart that covers a piece of paper and divide it into three sections, from top to bottom.

- In the bottom section, write down your greatest support.
- In the middle section, write down your greatest dream as a parent.
- In the top section, write down your greatest inspiration.

Put your heart somewhere where you can see it easily. Look at it every day and focus on each section of the heart. This will help it to become real.

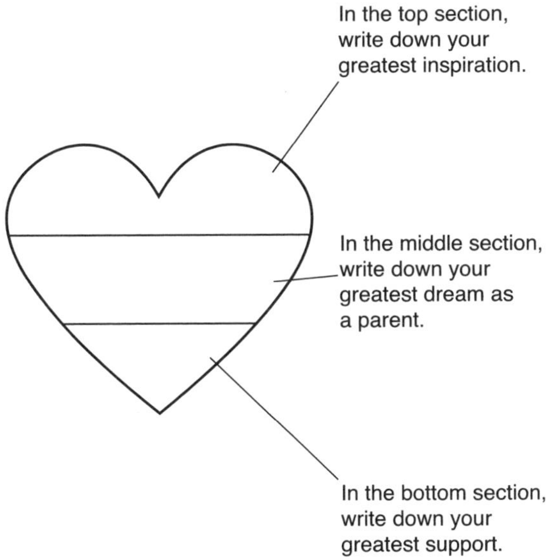

Your notes

USEFUL CONTACTS

Contact the author

Lorraine Thomas is Chief Executive of the Parent Coaching Academy. It offers:

- parent coach training for professionals
- resources for parents
- programmes for employers wanting to support parents in the workplace

www.theparentcoachingacademy.com
lthomas@theparentcoachingacademy.com

Support organisations

www.parentalk.co.uk
Parentalk is a national charity set up to inspire and motivate parents. It provides a wide range of resources for parents and professionals working with parents.

www.theamazinggroup.com
The Amazing Group produces a wide range of innovative interactive resources for parents and children including the following (on p. 242):

- **Feel Good Not Guilty About Being A Working Mum by Lorraine Thomas.**
  A resource for parents and employers wanting to support parents in the workplace. The programme provides short interactive sessions offering tools and techniques to deal with the Top 10 Challenges facing working mums.

- **Amazing People – The Teenage Years**
  A resource for parents wanting to support their children through school and exams.

www.mother@work.com
A monthly webzine dedicated to working mothers, offering advice and support on both practical and emotional issues.

www.bbc.co.uk/parenting
The BBC's parenting homepage, with a wealth of hints and tips from preconception to dealing with teenage tantrums.

RECOMMENDED READING

Annette Briley and Tim Mungeam, *The Parentalk Guide to the First Six Weeks* (Hodder & Stoughton, 2001)

Steve Chalke, *How to Succeed as a Parent* (Hodder & Stoughton, 2003)

Steve Chalke, *How to Succeed as a Working Parent* (Hodder & Stoughton, 2003)

Steve Chalke, *The Parentalk Guide to the Toddler Years* (Hodder & Stoughton, 1999)

Kate Daymond, *The Parentalk Guide to Sleep* (Hodder & Stoughton, 2001)

Adele Faber, *How to Talk So Kids Will Listen and Listen So Kids Will Talk* (Piccadilly Press, 2001)

Dr Christopher Green, *New Toddler Taming* (Vermilion, 2006)

Diane Louise Jordan, *How to Succeed as a Single Parent* (Hodder & Stoughton, 2003)

Lorraine Thomas, *The 7 Day Parent Coach* (Vermilion, 2005)